The Gr

Simulat

Parts 1 & 2

Your Practical Guide To Recognising The Amazing Illusion You Are Experiencing

By

David McCready

This paperback is published in Great Britain by:
McCready
Level 6
Tower 42
Old Broad St
London EC2N 1HN

www.GreatSimulator.com
Info@GreatSimulator.com

This is a first edition 2007

Principal Editor:
Roger J Gould

Copy Editor:
Greg Collins

Sketch supplied by:
Francisco Pena

Earth images supplied by:
NASA

ISBN 978-0-9557138-0-4

Printed and bound by:
Print On Demand
Graphic House
1 First Drove
Fengate
Peterborough PE1 5BJ

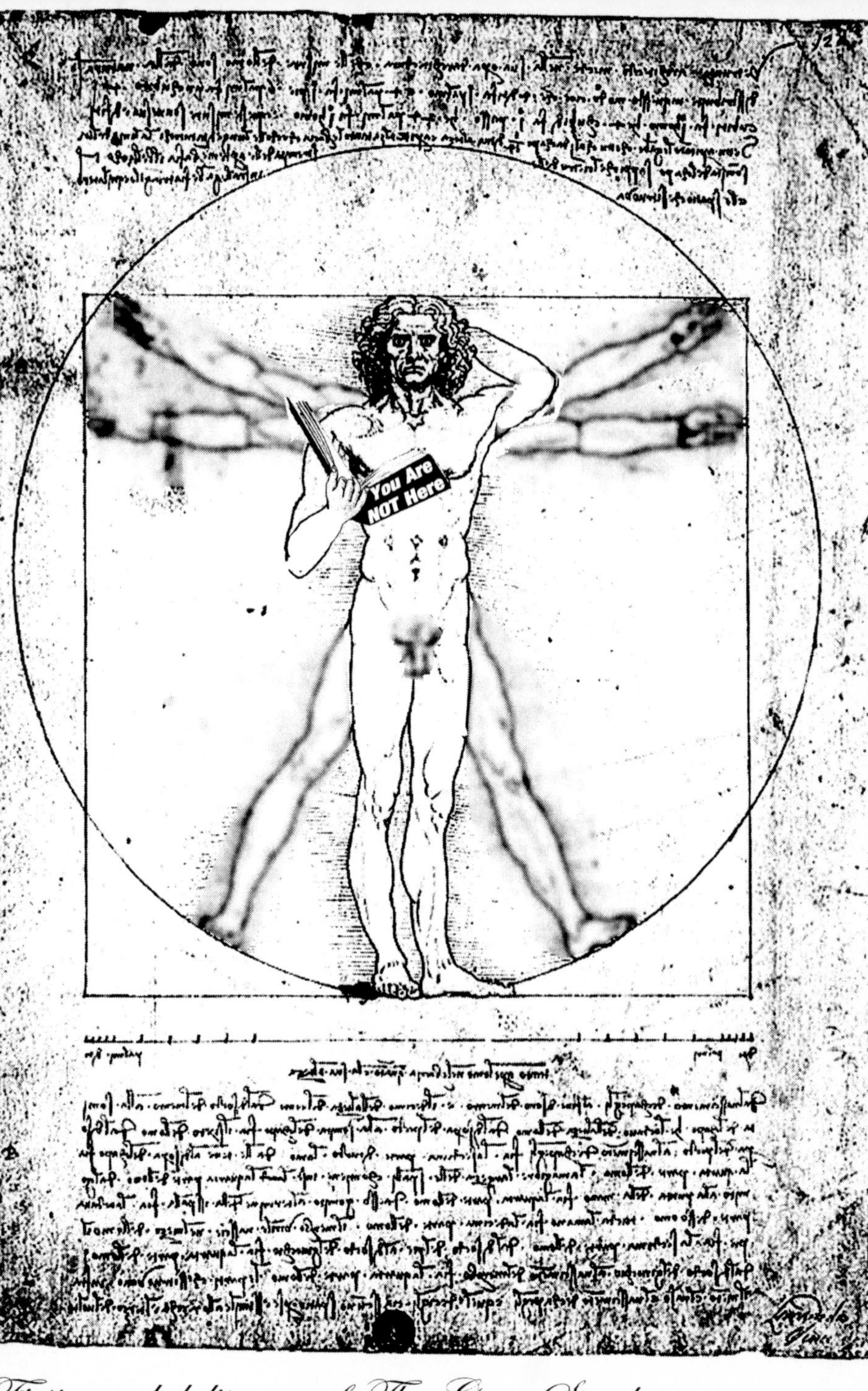

First recorded discovery of The Great Simulator manuscript

Background To This Book

19 September 2007

Dear Reader

Approximately ten years ago I ceased practicing my formal profession of engineering and building maintenance. I then took up the new, and difficult to precisely define, profession of helping people connect to their higher abilities.

Even to the date of writing this note to you, I still have no traditional definition of how to describe my work. Clients have commented that it appears to incorporate elements of psychology, neural linguistic programming, coaching, and spiritual awareness.

All I can really say about what I do is that it has achieved remarkable results for a great many people.

However, even more remarkable, and unusual, is the technology behind making significant advances in people's natural ability. The approach taken is not a philosophy, instead it is based on tried and tested empirical observations that have been successfully applied by my clients.

Ultimately, the secret to developing yourself is recognising that the real you is experiencing a magnificent and compelling illusion. In fact, the human being you may be inclined to think you are right now, does not really exist !

I hope you enjoy this book.

David

Chapters

Part 1

Part 2

Part 1

1 Introduction

Hello reader.

This book is a manual that is designed to give you an in-depth understanding of how to access your own Free Will.

At this point in your existence you will have noticed that "Life" does not always go the way you wanted it to.

Actually, "Life" is doing precisely what you wanted it to. But as what you wanted will appear to be hidden in your sub-conscious, you won't remember your real choices. In fact it is very difficult to remember because you are currently experiencing a most ingenious illusion.

To help you see through the illusion you are experiencing and hence regain access to your Free Will, you first need to recognise that you are in an illusion.

Example

Have you ever tried to repair a piece of mechanical equipment when you have little or no idea how it functions?

You might, for example, have found computers difficult and temperamental to operate. Or you may have been trying to fix a broken-down car.

When you know how something works and a fault arises it is easy to repair. Conversely, when you do not know how something works, it is often impossible to fix or maintain it.

The most complex piece of equipment you own is your human body. As you may have noticed, it was supplied without any operating instructions. Our conventional understanding of how it works is generally very limited, even for members of the medical profession.

The most difficult part of your body to understand is your mind. Even though you use your mind all the time, you will constantly encounter difficulties if you try to improve or change its performance.

How often have you wanted to be more energised, yet actually found yourself underperforming?

How often have you wanted to change your attitude towards something yet found it very difficult?

How many times has your ability to achieve something been limited by the apparent unwillingness of your mind and hence your body to cooperate?

My professional background is engineering but for the last decade I have devoted myself to improving the performance of human beings. In the course of helping people I have made an in-depth study of how we function and why we tend to behave the way we do. You could say that I have been developing a kind of "Human Operating Manual".

Human Operating Manual

The "Human Operating Manual" that I have been developing is designed to give you a practical understanding of how to get more from yourself and the people around you. So its many practical applications include:

- Your Job
- Your Relationships
- Your Health
- Your Creativity
- Your Happiness

I do not claim to have discovered the answer to everything. That is not what this book is about. This book was written to help you profoundly influence your ability to achieve measurable improvements in these areas.

Everyday Illusions

Now, imagine yourself sitting in a cinema.

Suppose you did not realise it was just a film being projected from a machine at the back of the theatre onto the screen in front of you. Everything you would be watching on the screen would appear to be:

- Very real
- Impossible to change

When you visit a cinema or movie theatre, you know you are watching an illusion. You know that to change the illusion you have to change the reel of film on the projection equipment.

But if no-one ever revealed to you that you were watching a powerful illusion, and you never noticed it for yourself, you might easily think that everything you saw was actually TOTALLY REAL.

Consciously influencing what is taking place in an illusion is made infinitely easier when you are not being fooled into taking it seriously. It is much easier to influence what is happening in an illusion when you can consciously recognise it for what it is. Similarly, to change your life, you need to be able to recognise the illusions you are experiencing in your own life.

The Illusion Of Life

The illusion almost every human being is experiencing works because, for a variety of reasons, you take it seriously. The Great Simulator works because you think it is real.

Your rational thought process and its accompanying imagination are key components in making the illusion of human life real. If you want to see the illusion taking place you have to stop contemplating what it "might be".

However, to start to see the illusion, you have to do something even more challenging and fundamental. You have to begin to recognise that you really did want to experience it in the first place.

Try and imagine everything you are experiencing right now is an illusion. You are not a prisoner of this illusion. You are willingly creating it. Therefore, everything that happens to you happens because you want it to.

You will find it hard to imagine this.

Hard, because you perceive yourself to be experiencing lots of things you cannot imagine yourself wanting to experience.

You perceive yourself to be a very real human entity with things happening to you in a somewhat random fashion. The truth is that this perception is corrupted and distorted. Yet you will tend to believe it to be real because you have little else to relate to. Understanding the way you perceive the world around you can have surprising and profound consequences.

Your human consciousness, which presently acts through the mechanism of your brain, is designed to make this illusion as real as possible. You cannot easily escape the illusion because you simply do not want to. You cannot just step out of the illusion you are in until you start to comprehend why you are in it in the first place.

How This Book Benefits You

This book is divided into two parts:

- **Part 1** is an outline of the illusion you are experiencing along with insights into how it is created.

- **Part 2** is a set of exercises that help you test the authenticity of what I have written for you. Applying them to the practical challenges you face will give you immediate benefits and life-changing improvements.

You could compare this book to a manual that tells you how to fly. The first part describes how your aeroplane works and describes flying. The second part tells you how to go about flying the plane for yourself. The basic principles are relatively straightforward. The skill is essentially a physical one rather than an intellectual one.

To become a pilot requires a great deal more than simply reading a manual. Pilots have to be trained by other pilots. It's a long, complicated and sometimes dangerous process. Fortunately, in the case of learning to see the illusion you are in, the worst that can happen is that you end up believing it is real. Ironically, that would be what you actually wanted, up to this point in your life anyway, but I'm getting ahead of myself.

There are two reasons why I wrote this book and why you will benefit from reading it:

1. Although you want to be in this illusion you also want to awaken from it.

2. Applying any of the exercises in this book, though they can be challenging, is likely to have a positive impact on your life.

For you to access your Free Will you have to notice what is really going on and that cannot be done until you "wake up". You are reading this because you want to make positive changes to your life and this book was created to help you succeed in "waking up".

Over the years I have taught many people how to gradually perceive the same surroundings in a new way. Many of them were people who wanted to do better in business. As these people overcame some of the illusions that limited them, they made rapid advances in both their work and many other areas of their lives.

Writing this book is an exciting experiment designed to give you a practical manual you can apply to everyday challenges. I hope you find it interesting reading, and as soon as you start applying what is written here physically, you will find it life-changing.

You are experiencing a fantastic adventure.

Welcome to The Great Simulator.

PS.

Whilst writing an earlier book I consistently found that I was spelling Earth as Earht. My computer's spell checker was persistently highlighting this error with its disapproving red lines. Yet I just kept on spelling it that way and then having to correct it. So in this book, I decided to let this alternative occur without alteration. This alternative spelling has provoked the wrath of my editors, who disapprove of this perversion of the English language. However, spelling Earth as Earht remains as a reminder to you that you are not really here.

2 All Back-To-Front

The easiest intellectual way to grasp on what is going on is to begin to recognise that virtually everything you are experiencing is…… back-to-front. Your whole existence is to a very large extent the opposite of how it appears to be.

Some books would take you gradually through a series of observations and the evidence behind them. However, with this book, a "fast track" approach has been adopted.

To learn how to see "The Great Simulator" in action for yourself you have to let go of many of your old concepts of what you think you are. Sometimes the process can be exciting, other times it can be frightening as many of your old certainties will have to be abandoned.

Significant Illusions Created By The Great Simulator

To help you make the transition between a "Flat Earth" model of your world to a "Round Earth" actuality, here are some examples of what you are likely to discover as you make your own exploration:

There is only one of us.

Even though there appear to be lots of us. This is an important part of the illusion. You are everyone which includes me. Harming others is harming yourself. Helping others is helping yourself. This book is a message from you, to you.

You are not here.

Whether you see this during your Earht life, or when your physical body dies, you WILL discover that you were never really alive on Earth. Instead you were just experiencing the strong illusion that you were a living human being. In fact one of the common problems experienced by the recently deceased is coming to terms with the fact that they were never really physically alive in the first place.

It's all pointless……. But there is a point.

Many people find a purpose in life through physical achievement. As you increase your awareness and recognise the illusion of life for what it is, such achievements will start to appear pointless. This recognition can potentially make you apathetic and hence incapacitate you. However, to embrace the real purpose of your human experience, it is a "bridge" you have to cross. To see your real purpose, you must first let go of many old perceptions and notions.

You want to experience this life.

This is one that many people have endless difficulty in accepting. The normal human attitude is that a "better life" of some sort is highly desirable. However, that completely denies any recognition of the fact that you appear to be very firmly locked into this one. So why are you giving yourself a life that appears to contain some "imperfections" ?

You are not your thoughts and emotions.

People tend to define themselves as the sum of the thoughts and emotions they experience. The greater reality is that none of them are the real you. Because these thoughts and emotions are so powerful and overwhelming, it is very difficult for a human being to recognise what it actually is.

The last point is really the heart of the matter. Fundamentally, just about everything you, the human being, perceive yourself to be is not actually you at all. Your experience of being a living, breathing, human being on Earth is just about as far from the greater reality as it is possible to get.

This is why relating to or recognising what you actually are can be so difficult. Your ongoing experience of living as a "Human Being" makes you tend to dismiss the truth of what you are. It is not even that the greater reality or truth is even hidden from you; you are just choosing not to recognise it. What you really are is so different to your perception of yourself, that you keep dismissing reality and remain in this amazing illusion.

This book is designed to help you notice things you had previously chosen to ignore. To use the cinema analogy, you have been so fixated by the action on the screen in front of you, you never really looked behind you at the projector.

Technical Insight

Not only has the "cinema screen" in front of you been made very interesting and compelling to follow, but the projector behind you has been cloaked in "apathy".

Your brain makes most of its decisions based on how you "feel" about a subject. When you have too many conflicting feelings your brain selectively ignores them until you are left with one clear and simplified feeling about what you want to think and do. This process is normally described as rationalising.

Your brain will often experience an apathy towards recognising the greater reality. Instead it is influenced by outside forces that make it want to focus on the illusion. You do not recognise the illusion for what it is because you allow yourself to be influenced not to do so.

It is that simple.

Advanced Thinking

Thinking about this is, ironically, creating a continuance of the illusion you are experiencing. Trying to work any of this out in your mind is futile, as your brain is designed to make the illusion you are experiencing very real. To recognise the illusion you need to use your Advanced Thinking ability.

Advanced Thinking is actually the art of not really thinking at all, in the traditional sense. You still use the processing capacity of your brain, but you avoid most of its rationalising function. When you rationalise, you dismiss apparently irrelevant information. When you are being aware, you take in everything. Reality turns out to have been disguised as irrelevance and further camouflaged in apathy.

When you ignore your Advanced Thinking ability, you will experience disinterest and extreme difficulty in recognising what is happening. But you will probably complain, incorrectly, that much of what happens to you is against your will.

People who demonstrate an Advanced Thinking ability are in no way superior to those who rarely do. Everyone is equal. Advanced Thinking is something you will already have experienced. When you follow the exercises in the second part of this book you will experience it more often.

The truth is all around you.

Everyday Illusions

Your brain is pre-programmed to keep making sense of the world it perceives. As it has learnt to willingly dismiss nearly any sense it has of the Greater Reality almost anything becomes believable.

You are largely living in a world of "mental models". Even what you see with your eyes has been adjusted:

- Example; the lens mechanism in your eye ball sees everything upside down. Your brain has adjusted this to be the right way up.
- Example; your eye balls each have "blind spots". You do not normally notice this because your brain has "filled in" the gaps in your vision with what it thinks is there.
- Example; your brain only receives electro chemical signals from your eyes. From this it constructs an imaginary image of the physical world. Everything your eyes physically see has to be imagined by your brain.
- Sometimes your brain ignores the electro chemical signals from your eyes altogether and imagines other things. So you literally do not see what is in front of you. This is how, for example, many car crashes occur.

The combined effect of your brain being so busy making sense of things, imagining other things, while ignoring nearly everything, is to create a very dubious sense of reality. As your brain is also normally apathetic towards the greater reality but, conversely, enthusiastic towards perceived excitement, it is very easily fooled.

You gain most of your human sense of identity based on the perceptions of your brain. Hence, you are basing most of your sense of identity on corrupted and incomplete information, plus fantasies about what you perceive yourself to be.

Back-To-Front

Overall, your entire human existence is a fantastically well engineered and convincing illusion that has turned reality "back to front". As you will discover, nearly everything you are experiencing is not real, but has been constructed in a way that the human brain perceives as real.

Yet from this strange predicament, we do have a useful tool which will help us uncover the truth. Many of the mysteries we face in our lives are insoluble because significant elements such as the purpose of our lives frequently do not "make sense". This is because the illusion you are experiencing has caused you to arrive at false assumptions.

To overcome the false assumptions you are making, you simply have to use your Advanced Thinking ability. Whenever you use this higher awareness you will be open to recognising the incredible reversal of reality we call Earth.

A simple example of what you will discover is as follows. Whilst reading this book, a typical person will sense himself/herself to be a consciousness looking out through a pair of eyes. The reality is that it would be more accurate to say that you are everything else apart from that consciousness behind the pair of eyes. How back-to-front and initially difficult to grasp is that ?

3 The Help Around You

You Are Not Alone

One impression that most people often have in life is the sense of sometimes being alone.

You, the Earht consciousness, are never alone. Your "spirit friends" are always with you.

Some people will have already recognised this. Some people will relate to these "friends" as guiding spirits, others will see them as deceased relatives come to help. There are a multitude of interpretations you can apply to this. Furthermore, depending on where you are focused, the "local reality" can appear to be different. Meanwhile you, the human consciousness, never were alone and you never will be.

How This Is Achieved

At the risk of confusing you, earlier I pointed out that there is really only one of us. But at the Earht level there will appear to be many of us. So I will appear to be separate from you. This allows for separate consciousnesses to appear to exist. This mechanism makes it possible to create different people. You might say that we are all formed from the same material but in individual ways. It's a fantastic way to create a really interesting illusion. It also means that you, the human consciousness, are never alone.

What I am about to describe next, most people will try to imagine, and will imagine incorrectly at that. So let this act as a rough guide until you experience it for yourself. You are guaranteed to experience the greater reality because, at some point, your physical form will die. If you experience it before then, that is even better. Inaccurate imagination is, therefore, in the meantime, temporarily excused. As I just said, when you try to imagine this you will get it "wrong". But don't worry, this section is just here to inform you.

The concept to grasp is that you, the human consciousness, actually do not look like a human being at all. More like a ball of energy. A ball of energy with no defined edge. So it is not clear where you start or finish.

Meanwhile you relate to yourself as something with defined boundaries. As this is what you relate to, anything trying to communicate with you will often, helpfully, give itself the appearance of defined boundaries. Therefore a guiding spirit will tend to appear to you as human or angelic, with defined boundaries, in order not to confuse you.

So here is a picture that is not quite accurate, but at least gives you some clue as to what is going on. You look like a ball of energy floating in a dark space. There are other balls of energy around you, who could loosely be called your guiding spirits or Guides. Some of them will be known to you as deceased relatives. Others could simply be considered spirit friends who you will never physically recognise during this Earht life.

As I explained, you tend to see yourself as a human being and your Guides will also tend to appear as human beings, because that is what you relate to. In some cultures people will often see Guides as animals, it does not really matter. Guides like to give you a familiar point of reference. A deceased relative such as a grandmother will normally appear looking old because that is what you relate to. If she were to appear to you as a bouncing

16 year old you would not necessarily relate to her, or recognise her, as being you grandmother.

Meanwhile, to our guiding spirits, you will appear to be more like that ball of light, which is under the impression that it is a human being. If a guiding spirit wanted to communicate with you it would merely be a matter of blending in with your energy. This often has the physical effect of making you feel cold, or experience a chilling shiver. To communicate with you, requires "borrowing" some of your Earht form to some extent, and you may experience this temporary "loss" as a cold sensation.

Mission Control

Guiding spirits are there to help you. If you were an astronaut, they would be your mission control on the ground. They can assist you in a variety of ways if you let them do so.

The big confusion that generally arises is that many people think that their Guides are there to solve all their Earhtly problems. Guides on the other hand see it very differently. You are experiencing the Earht plane of "The Great Simulator" because you wanted to. You wanted to experience various challenges. It would be most unhelpful of your Guides just to intervene to take away all your problems, when you actually wanted those same problems in the first place. Even if, whilst in your human form, you don't consciously remember this and ask them to solve that "problem" for you.

What Guides do well is to help you raise your awareness. When you raise your awareness you tend to see the solution to your problems. After all, that is ultimately what you wanted to do.

The classic mistake is to complain that your Guides are not helping you enough or even at all. This lowers your awareness and in turn makes it harder for your Guides to assist you. So the more you complain that you are not being helped enough, the less help you are able to receive.

I have frequently encountered clients who have become angry with their Guides. Fortunately, the Guides never appear troubled by such attitudes and peacefully await the return of "common sense". Clients, on the other hand, do not initially recognise that to be angry at Guides means connecting to "darker forces". This discovery can often be quite shocking for them.

Practical Help

The great advantage of having guiding spirits is that they can assist you in a very wide variety of ways. They can assist you to exhibit skills you would not otherwise possess. You can "chat" with them. They can help you heal yourself and others. They also help you access the energy and drive to perform great feats or tasks. There are many possibilities.

In my case, I wanted to learn how to connect with the Greater Reality beyond the illusion I was experiencing, though I would have described it to you differently at the time. However, I was, for the most part, lacking suitable human Earhtly assistance, so I was instead made aware of the idea that my guiding spirits existed and they could help me develop. They did, and I acquired skills that were not obviously available through other human beings around me.

What I did is not actually that unique, you only have to look around you to see individuals who appear to have developed skills and acquired knowledge apparently on their own. What was more unusual was that I was aware to some extent of how I was doing it. Your Guides have already and will continue to support you.

What Are Guides

Ultimately, there is only one of us so you are your Guides anyway. But at the Earht level, they will appear to be separate from you.

Guides can also appear to be in two places at once. So two or more people can connect to them in different parts of the world at any time and have different "conversations".

You also tend to influence how they communicate with you, which is where more confusion can arise. If you want to "hear" something from them, you probably will appear to do so. But you could easily be fooling yourself. You have to be very impartial to get a good "accurate" link.

There are plenty of other spirit forms out there that I would not classify as Guides. In fact some of them appear to exist principally in order to confuse unwary humans. To begin with you will normally experience some difficulty in telling the difference. Your normal thinking rationalising thought process makes you particularly susceptible to their influence. However, the fact that you are reading this means that they have not killed you yet.

Guides are there to give you your more advanced abilities and awareness. To a large extent you could call them "Stage Managers". What you perceive yourself to be is to a large extent a restricted combination of their combined consciousnesses plus some other things.

You are not limited to communicating with Guides / spirit friends or relatives, etc. Any of the "prophets" are generally available; Moses, Abraham, Jesus, Mohammed, Buddha, Krishna, etc. But note that there are a great deal of spirit forms out there that masquerade as these prophets, so later on I will give you a few tips on how to tell the difference.

Expand Your Awareness

Meanwhile, there is one important tip that you should be aware of immediately. Whilst this book is for the most part a limited technical description of a magnificent creation, you will benefit from moving your understanding of what is being described beyond the limitations of your intellect. Instead, you need to use the awareness of your Guides.

The reason for doing so is simplicity itself. Your intellect is an active component in the manifestation of the illusion you are experiencing. Hence, you cannot think, intellectualise, or rationalise your way out of it. Your Guides, on the other hand, do not possess intellects, and are therefore not bound by the consequential illusion.

To demonstrate a higher level of consciousness and truly recognise the illusion you are experiencing demands that you must acquire a higher awareness. For you to achieve this at some stage requires you to familiarise yourself with your guiding spirits and share their higher awareness.

When you do recognise the presence of your guiding spirits, you are also in a position to experience a wonderful unconditional love. As humans, we have many fears, so we need to recognise that our Guides, who only have a wonderful unconditional love for you, are not going to harm you. Feeling this unconditional love is one of the means you have of determining that you have indeed connected with the higher awareness of your guiding spirits.

The essential point about life in The Great Simulator is that you are never alone. Someone or something is always watching you. You have no privacy. Everything you do can be, and is always seen. Similarly, you are constantly receiving an enormous degree of "help".

You may be judgemental and divide your actions into "Good" or "Bad" categories. Your Guides do not do that. They are not under any illusions that gives purpose to being judgemental. So when you communicate with them, remember that you will inevitably have a distorted view of the Earht, whilst your Guides will see it for what it is. This is one reason why their unconditional love does not appear blocked by judgmental attitudes.

Allow them to help you to expand your awareness. For you to have a greater influence on what happens in your life, you need to comprehend what is actually happening right now.

Incidentally, whilst this description of The Great Simulator describes your Guides in terms which suggests them to be separate entities from you, that is a mild inaccuracy. In practice there is only one of us anyway. So if you perceive them to be somehow (perhaps) smarter aspects of yourself that is entirely understandable.

4 Astral World

As long as man has lived on Earht, it has generally been a belief that there is another world of some sort. Many people subscribe to the idea of heaven. Some even have the additional concept of hell, and for a dwindling few there is also a purgatory. However, all religions and, in practice, the majority of people subscribe to the idea that there is probably some sort of "afterlife".

The confusion arises in that, for most people, there is no obvious access to this other world. Occasionally, people who have died are revived and are returned to life, some of whom retain the memory of what happened on the "other side". The experience of what happens on the "other side" tends to be similar for people globally, regardless of location or culture. Something appears to happen, but it can be hard to know exactly what is going on "on the other side". To reduce this confusion, this series of books contain exercises that enable you to explore the "other side" without the need for a "near-death experience".

Exploring The Astral World

Meanwhile, some people have found methods of getting back to the "other side" or, as it is more commonly referred to by those who have consciously been there, The Astral or The Astral World. Meditation techniques are very effective in this respect and with practice you can experience some of the Astral World without the need to have a near-death experience.

Some professional hypnotists have also found that if you regress patients under hypnosis, you can recover memories of this Astral "other world". It is similarly possible to recover memories of previous existences and other things not normally found in your conscious mind.

It is possible to explore the Astral World consciously. However, for the typical reader of this book it is very difficult to do so consciously. The simple reason why you will not is that your desire to believe that the Earht is real is so strong you are afraid to "project" away. You are restrained by a deep subconscious fear of death. Leaving your body is associated with death and that fear prevents you consciously projecting onto the Astral.

Obviously, if you saw this Astral World for yourself, you would instantly understand the basis upon which The Great Simulator was written. However, as you have a strong unconscious desire to believe that The Great Simulator is real and the part you are experiencing is called planet Earth, you will encounter obstacles. Hence it is initially difficult to lose that subconscious fear of death.

Yet you actually do experience parts of the Astral World on a daily basis. This book will help you recognize the parts of it that you are already conscious of, but probably ignoring. Through this approach it is actually easier to explore the Astral World than it may first appear. The next difficulty faced by most people is that it often appears to be so different, that they think they have not found it and have instead made some sort of mistake in trying to get there. So in this chapter, we are looking at some aspects of what the Astral World is like, in order to familiarize you.

Navigating The Simulator

The simulation of life and consciousness you are experiencing is but a small part of something much bigger. Anyone familiar with the subject of Astral Projection will be familiar with the practicalities of projecting your consciousness out of your body so that you can visit other places. The techniques that help you do this are covered later on in Part 2 of this book. Though it is worth noticing that you already perform unconscious Astral Projection every time you sleep.

Anyone who has developed the ability to consciously perform Astral Projection will have discovered that (let's call it) the Earht plane is but one of many dimensions. Dimensions are worlds that essentially overlap. So, the Astral World is comprised of many sub-worlds or planes that essentially all exist in the same place. It is therefore possible to move between one and another almost instantly, once you have remembered how it is done.

Most people experiencing human life will have blocked out their memory of how to navigate within the Astral World simply to make the human experience more compelling and realistic. For example, on Earht there are good reasons for fearing death, yet you would instantly lose that fear if you were to see everyone who had ever died, alive and well in another dimension. For your "own stability" you have probably blocked out most of your understanding of how to navigate the Astral World; completely losing your fear of death could result in you prematurely exiting the Earht plane. So you retain that fear to help keep your physical body alive.

For simplicity you could divide the Astral World into the high vibration/energy levels and the low vibration/energy levels.

High Levels

- Everything is very connected.
- You will experience a oneness.
- Time ceases to exist.
- You have little or no individuality.

Low Levels

- Time starts to exist the lower you go.
- There is a higher degree of separation between things.
- You can experience individuality: i.e. differences between you and other things.
- Physical solidity is becoming possible.

Earht Level

- This is about as low as you can go in the Astral World
- Sometimes confused with Hell, which is truly a figment of our imaginations.
- Time is very real.
- Distances now exist and take time to traverse.
- Everything is very solid.
- The "oneness" is mostly now obscured.
- Welcome back to Earth

The Way It Is

Now another human confusion starts to arise if you choose to believe the concept that "one thing" might be better than "another thing". For example, you might believe that it is better to live in the High Astral than the Low Astral. This completely ignores the fact that you wanted to experience the Low Astral and in particular the Earht dimension in the first place. This idea that "one thing" might be better than "another thing" is one of the mechanisms you employ to keep yourself within the Earht plane of the Low Astral, even though you will think that you want to be on the High Astral.

The Astral World is the main part of The Great Simulator you are experiencing. It is a series of different dimensions, and associated sub-worlds or realms where your consciousness can exist. So to keep this simple enough to comprehend, understand that your consciousness is an invention and it only appears to exist in the Astral World. You, the human consciousness, are currently experiencing a sub-world called the Earht plane.

Whilst reading this book your consciousness will appear to mostly exist on the Earht plane and, in particular, inside your head. But your total consciousness also exists throughout the Astral World. The reality is that it is not focused at all. It just appears to be focused, in order to make the illusion, you are in, appear real enough to be convincing.

By increasing your awareness, and losing your subconscious fear of death you can project your consciousness around the Astral world. For example, you wanted to find your deceased human relatives, your yet-to-be-conceived children, or anyone else, just tour the Astral World and you will find them. Though please be aware that they do not necessarily appear in Human form, which might confuse you a little to begin with.

God

Could you find God ?

Yes and No is actually a great answer.

You are a part of God. Everything else on the Astral is part of God. Your difficulty in finding God would be establishing a point, or focused singularity, called God. Put another way, it is difficult to find God, because God is not a single spot (or person) you could call God. The Astral world is infinitely small, yet designed to appear infinitely large to a human consciousness. So you will tend to experience your consciousness as a small entity looking for an enormous entity called God which is in fact all around you and part of you.

So to look for God, you first have to ignore God. Which is why you cannot find God if you are looking for God, because you would be ignoring the obvious presence of God. However, God would not have much difficulty in making its presence known to you if it chose to, which if you pay attention, it does. I hope that is clear and easy to understand.

Heaven & Hell

Heaven is another place people go looking for. There are a number of versions of human heaven on the Astral and because of this there are some conflicting reports as to exactly what Heaven is like.

The types of human heaven you will find broadly fall into two types:

1. There are the heavens for human consciousnesses still under the illusion that they are human. These ones will resemble the traditional concepts of heaven and they have some Earhtly features. Typically they have city-like features and many places of rest and worship; being relatively solid, they are also easier for you to recognize.

2. Then there are the heavens for human consciousnesses who recognized that they were never human at all. It is not really fair to define these planes as particularly distinct from the rest of the Astral as they are inherently formless. The consciousnesses there are happy to exist in a state of oneness that eliminates separation and hence any form of distinct boundaries. This part of the Astral is easy to reach, but will be uninteresting to most human consciousnesses as it is somewhat featureless.

Conversely, it is difficult to find Hell. There are some localized "spots" that look "Hell-like", but on examination they are created by consciousnesses who desire that experience. Furthermore, such "spots" are lacking solid physical form and therefore physical pain. "A good roasting by demons" is not a practicality, as the experience would be no worse than a brief nightmare, with no real pain. What's more, as you are choosing where you are going, nothing can actually send you anywhere, especially to "Hell". To experience physical suffering you really need to be experiencing the Earht plane and you already know all about that.

Other Consciousnesses

The Astral World will appear to contain lots of other consciousnesses as part of the great simulation you are experiencing. Many of these consciousnesses are actually forming your human consciousness.

One of the essential features of the illusion you are experiencing is that you will tend to identify yourself as being one unique human consciousness. The reality is the complete opposite of that. The feeling you experience of being "you" is made up of lots of little feelings that pass through "you" from one moment to the next. On the Astral you can see this happening, whilst on Earht you will normally be wondering "what has happened".

The point of this book is to help you recognize that the "person" you think you are does not actually exist. You are in fact something completely different. On Earht you are only experiencing being a human being/consciousness. When you start to explore the Astral World you start to see how a human consciousness is actively formed moment by moment. But whilst you are fully absorbed experiencing being a human consciousness on Earht, you do not easily recognize what you are.

What You Are

Ultimately there is only one of us. One of us that will appear to have broken itself into lots of little bits. So you and I (the writer) are actually the same entity. But in the Low Astral I will appear to be completely separate from you. This makes it possible for you to read a book that appears to have been written by someone else.

I say "appears", because ultimately there has not been a separation. The illusion of a separation is created in The Astral World and particularly, in low regions such as the Earht plane which you currently are experiencing.

You will appear to be constructed from lots of bits, both large and small, of consciousnesses living in the Astral World. Now when it comes time to form a human consciousness, the being you think you are, lots of these elements are assembled.

The result is a bit like a football team thinking that it is one person. All the individual members of the team would still each experience their own personal identity, but the combined team (you) would have a consciousness that sees itself as one (not many) individual.

The Great Simulator makes it possible for an artificial construction (you) to think it has a consciousness. Hence it can believe it exists as something which is actually entirely different from what it really is. For this artificial construction (you) to have Free Will, it has to recognize what it is. Therefore, for you to have Free Will, you need to first recognize what you are NOT. Then you will start to notice what you actually are.

Components & Layers

A human consciousness is constructed from a multitude of components or bits. Some are "high vibration or energy" and some are "low vibration or energy", with lots of intermediate "vibration or energy" states in between. You could say that these components, or bits, are like layers of an onion.

When your human body physically dies, you will see the "layers" of different spirit / energy forms that compose it stripped away. As the low vibration / energy layers are dispensed with you will experience "floating" up to heaven.

Incidentally, if you tried to prevent this stripping / dispensing process you would find yourself "Earth Bound" as a ghost for a while. You would remain a ghost until the human illusion sufficiently wore off, and thus, eventually, you would let go of some these Earhtly characteristics and return to heaven.

Conversely, when you are conceived and finally get born as a human being, you will see all the components necessary to create the impression of human existence being gathered and blended together. Some people liken the experience as similar to being poured down a funnel.

The final part of the birth process comes when your human body emerges from its mother's womb and you get your "amnesia". Some degree of amnesia or loss of awareness is vital, otherwise you would instantly recognize the illusion for what it is. So, writing from personal experience, one of the first thoughts of a new baby is; "What happened ?"

Once on Earht your human consciousness then tends to remain in a state of ignorance as to what it actually is. This is, of course, an essential part of the design. However, to demonstrate any Free Will, this ignorance, as to what you actually are, is something that ultimately has to be rectified.

A good reason for learning to navigate the Astral World consciously, as opposed to the unconscious journeys you make every time you sleep, is for you to experience a greater reality. Hence, you will recognize what is actually happening. If you are hoping to make "improvements" to your Earht life, you first need to discover why your life already is the way it is now.

Your human form is actually an advanced machine made of various components and layers. If you really want it to perform differently, then it is essential that you recognize what it actually is and how it functions. Advancing your awareness of what you are experiencing is only really possible if you consciously access the Astral World.

Already On The Astral

It is actually much easier to do "Astral Projection" or "travelling" than you might think. The main difficulty is that you don't readily recognize what you are. In particular, at this moment, you are actually spending most of your time imagining that you are a living human being. Because you think in terms of "I am a human being", you tend not to recognize things that do not appear to be human or Earhtly.

Most of the spirit / energy forms that comprise a human consciousness do not look human at all. An analogy would be if you were to dismantle a green apple by placing it in a blender. The result would be a puddle of green slime; all the components of the green apple would be present, but it would no longer appear to be an apple.

Similarly, when experiencing the Astral World, the vast bulk of it is radically different to the Earht plane. So, instead of recognizing where you actually are, you will instead tend to start imagining your human world, and end up back "in your head".

The greater reality at this very moment is that you are already on the Astral, but you are imagining you are on Earht. You are imagining you are on the Earht because you, the super-consciousness, want to.

The Astral World is actually all around you right now, but you do not recognize it because it is so alien to what you expect it to be. That is why, for example, heaven (well the many heavens) had to be constructed. Human consciousnesses returning from the illusion of the Earht plane tend not to recognize where they actually are and so have a tendency to want to return to the Earht plane or something similar. Hence, the human heavens were constructed with some Earhtly features which are attractive to anything that wishes to continue imagining itself to be a human being.

To some extent, if you remember your nocturnal dreams, you can see the same process happening. When you dream, you will constantly be making sense of things in human terms. You will make everything appear human(ish). Even though much of your dreaming is in many ways "interesting nonsense", you will actively want to make "human" sense of it.

In many ways dying is like waking up from a nonsense dream. As you awaken you recognize what you were really experiencing. So, this awakening experience is something you should already be familiar with when you get up in the morning. A similar, but more profound experience, awaits you when your physical form dies.

Obviously then, practicing Astral Projection is a good and rather less terminal alternative to the awakening of physical death. But you are not going to allow yourself to discover how easy it is to consciously do "Astral Projection" until you address your greater overriding intention to experience the Earht plane. A more comprehensive explanation of how to do this is in Part 2 of this book.

Meanwhile, if you remember your dreams, you will already have experienced a significant degree of "Astral Projection" in the "Low Astral". If you have managed to become conscious that you are dreaming whilst asleep you will have noticed that you can "make up the rules" and define or change your dream. Hence in a very limited way, you would experience an early stage of manifesting Free Will.

Recognizing that you are in a nocturnal dream also offers you other interesting possibilities. In particular, you can escape your dream realm and move into the greater part of the Astral World.

One indication that you have moved beyond the "Low Astral Mini-world" of your dreams is that you become aware of other "Local Realities". You will find that these "Local Realities" or other "Mini-worlds" are created by other consciousnesses and you will be able to influence what you find.

You will also then be in a position to "go up" in the Astral where you will tend to find that these various worlds become larger and progressively less physically defined. Conversely, when you then return to the human "Mini-world" of the Earht plane, it can look surprisingly small when viewed from an Astral perspective.

Summary

These descriptions should help anyone who has not experienced conscious Astral Projection recognize that you really need to do it for yourself to comprehend what is being described here. The Astral World has many dimensions and most people will not currently relate to, or even recognize most of them.

By following the exercises in Part 2 of this book you will experience Astral Projection. Though, the emphasis is on getting you to recognize where you actually are now and hence assist you in manifesting some Free Will. For a fuller explanation into exploring the Astral World in general, you will find it in Part 3.

I have taught many of my clients to see auras, chat with their Guides and human relatives. So if you think you can't, stop fooling yourself; you are already on the Astral and you can do it too.

From now on begin to pay attention to the Astral World all around and within you. By this means you can progressively notice how you imagine yourself to be a human being on Earht.

Our next step in extracting you from this illusion is to deepen your understanding of the components that make up the impression of your human consciousness.

5 Special Effects Team

Not a single thought you have is actually yours. None of the emotions you experience in your human form are you. Yet, you walk around identifying yourself as these same thoughts and emotions.

The design of this is outstandingly clever. Everything you are inclined to think you are, you are not. Even thinking about this, right now, is part of the illusion you are in. You do, however, experience aspects of what you actually are; but as to what you are is obscured by an avalanche of other senses and, in particular, thoughts that are driven by Earhtly feelings, you will seldom recognise your true self.

To be aware of yourself requires learning the practical skill of Advanced Thinking, which in truth is not really thinking at all in the traditional sense. When you use your Advanced Thinking ability, you are in a position to be aware of how easily the thoughts you are experiencing are manipulated by "outside forces".

How You Have Negative Emotions

Previously we looked into the subject of Guiding Spirits, the ones who are there to help you be wise, aware of yourself, make good decisions, etc. So how then do you manage to experience:

- Making stupid decisions.
- Getting angry and upset.
- Wishing harm upon others.
- Having sexual thoughts.
- Daydreaming.

- Fear.
- Hope.
- Despair.
- Contemplating plans and ideas.

You are regularly experiencing a wide range of thoughts and emotions that are simply not possible if you were just influenced by your guiding spirits.

When you use your Advanced Thinking ability and practice being aware of yourself, you will start to notice how your human consciousness is influenced by a wide range of "lesser" spirit beings. In a number of philosophies, SOME (not all), of these "lesser" spirit beings are, occasionally, described as "evil spirits". Actually that is neither an accurate, nor even a fair, description of what they really are. For example, for you to experience sexual thoughts, your consciousness must become dominated by some of these spirit beings. If no one had any sexual thoughts the human race would become rapidly extinct, so they do have some practical purpose.

Lower Spirits

Once people become aware that they are indeed influenced by a range of spirit beings, they usually experience fear and try to somehow block them out. This strategy never works as you have chosen to experience their influence. Anyway, the fear emotion that would be inspiring you try to and block them out could only be supplied by these same spirit beings and, therefore, the whole exercise would be futile from the start.

If you want a quick demonstration of how your human consciousness is completely dominated by them, close your eyes and try to effortlessly:

- Have a clear head.
- Think about nothing.
- Stop imagining pictures.
- Don't talk to yourself with your thoughts.
- Have a relaxed content emotional state.

You can probably do this for a few seconds by concentrating very hard. But once your concentration lapses, which it will, you will soon return to the noisy internal conversation you normally experience. This experiment is designed to help you notice how your head is constantly permeated with thoughts, feelings and images. Thoughts, feelings and images that you appear to have no easy way of "turning off".

Later on I will give you an approach that allows you to "switch off the noise" by becoming aware of these spirit beings. Whenever you recognise, lovingly, that they are not you, they stop dominating you. What we are doing right now is establishing that your consciousness is dominated by spirit beings who cause you to experience a wide range of thoughts, emotions and images of a very "human" nature.

How we would see the spirit beings that do this depends on our point of view. Some people would see them as energy forms. In other situations they can seem to be small human-like creatures, perhaps with some animal-like characteristics. On top of that, they appear to come in an infinite range of shapes and sizes. You do not see them on the Earht plane as they do not exist here, but they are readily visible in the Astral World.

Addiction & Abilities

During the course of my professional work I have had the opportunity to assist people with addictions. I consistently found that such people always had a particular category of spirit entity influencing their human consciousness. Consequently, when meeting my clients I could determine their level of progress by simply looking at the degree of attachment they had to this category of spirit entity. A highly attached entity would immediately indicate that the addiction was very strong or conversely, when the attachment reduced, so would the addiction.

To give you a visual example, I have personally found addicts to have a particular shade of yellow in their auras. Similarly, the spirit entities influencing them could be likened to talkative parrots or monkeys on their shoulders. You can observe these lower spirit entities were influencing the addictive wants and desires of their human hosts.

Alternatively, if a client wished for a greater sexual drive or passion, they needed to learn how to encourage some "nymph" spirits to ferment the required thoughts and feelings. It is merely a matter of working with the forces needed to achieve a desired outcome.

If you wanted to become "smarter" there are simple techniques that allow you to experience more of a connection with your guiding spirits. However, here is the interesting part, your guiding spirits have to operate through these "lesser" spirits. So there is simply no way of, and actually no point in, getting rid of these spirits. To appear to be "smarter" requires a good link with your guiding spirits and, consciously or unconsciously, working with these "lesser" or "lower" spirits which form the building blocks of your human consciousness.

You Are A Genius

Ultimately, you are a genius. At the Earht level you will not have chosen to display all your ability. To create the genuine impression that you are not a genius is achieved by you "being something different". By ignoring any sense of what you really are, you can then identify yourself as a human being that is often trying to be "smarter". The "lesser" or "lower" spirit beings you are reading about make it possible for you to not be a genius by skilfully helping you block yourself.

At this point in a conversation, most people tend to entertain the thought that they are geniuses. However, at the risk of confusing you a little (read this section again if you have to), thinking that you are a genius will never make you a genius. Why? Because the thinking machine you are experiencing being is designed to be very limited. So obviously, a limited thinking machine, thinking it is a genius, has to be a fantasy.

To experience your true genius and display some amazing abilities, you have to stop thinking and fantasising. Instead you have to recognise the greater reality. You need to move beyond your limiting thoughts and emotions. By truly recognising how thoughts and emotions are an illusion, this becomes far easier. It is not enough just to think that they are illusion. If you don't believe me, just notice how thinking that you are a genius has little impact on your ability.

Working With The Team

One of the primary ways in which the "special effects team" of spirits help you experience the illusion you are in is by keeping you attention occupied. People who have acquired the skill to do deep and stable meditation can transcend this distraction with ease. However, the average person who reads this book will never have developed the capacity for that degree of clarity. This series of books gives you practical techniques that you are capable of applying to succeed in the challenge of seeing through the illusion you are experiencing.

The special effects team skilfully make you believe that you are something you are not. They are so skilful in their work that most human beings have no recollection of where they came from before they were conceived, or where they will be going when their physical bodies die. Some even deny that there could possibly be anywhere else except the physical Earth.

Don't fight the "special effects team" of spirits that make the illusion you are experiencing function. To do so merely makes the illusion stronger. The technique we will look into later involves congratulating them for the truly excellent job they do.

In the meantime, observe the degree to which you are not really in control of yourself. Notice the degree to which you react to situations in a very predictable way. You might be inclined to say that such behaviour is your character or nature. Yet if you want to change what you are and access many of your greater practical abilities, you need to transcend what you previously would have considered to be your character or nature.

By truly recognising that you are not the character you will have previously perceived yourself to be, you can make substantial changes with minimal real effort.

6 Movie Time

Here is a list of three simple means by which you are given the opportunity to fool yourself into believing that the world around you is actually real.

1. Get lots of people to believe it.

The degree to which human beings enjoy illusions is incredible. Yet, once everyone is doing it, it appears normal in an "everyday" sense. When everyone around you subscribes to the same illusion, you will tend to subscribe to it, unless you make a conscious effort not to. That is why, for example, most people find the experience of watching a film in a cinema is generally more vivid than doing so at home on your own.

In our human forms, because we are invisibly connected, we tend to experience similar emotions at the same time. For example, notice how when someone in your company is very happy or angry, this emotion is infectious. You cannot see the emotions physically, though you would on the Astral where they appear to be like clouds of energy that affect multiple consciousnesses.

When enough people believe something to be true, it becomes "true", for a while anyway. Thus, one of the mechanism's The Great Simulator uses to achieve a believable illusion is to have lots of people subscribing to the belief that the Earth really exists. Our Earth exists to us because we wanted it to.

2. The power of distraction.

The next amazingly effective mechanism that enables this illusion is the power of distraction. Anyone familiar with Illusionist Magic will know that the easiest way to create an illusion is to distract you from the "Real Action"

It is virtually impossible for the average human being to walk down the street just noticing where he or she is without significant distraction:

- You think about and, normally, visualise conversations you have had.
- You think about and, normally, visualise conversations you will have.
- You wonder what other people did, do or will think about you.
- You entertain memories and fantasises.
- Most people also enjoy watching television and relaxing in front of the various visual illusions. They are deliberately not noticing where they are.
- Most people enjoy reading news or stories that inspire new images or fantasises in their heads. Again, they are deliberately not noticing where they are.

A truly unusual sight is to find a human being happily noticing where he or she is, without digressing into a fantasy of some sort.

It is amazing that despite such a high degree of distraction you do not, regularly, collide with lampposts or passing vehicles.

Not only do you have a predisposition towards wanting to experience fantasies, you also appear to want them to be of the highest quality. The annual Hollywood Oscar ceremony is a celebration of making something that never was real almost appear totally real. Actors are given awards for making you believe that they were real characters and not actors. Special effects specialists are rewarded for creating believable computer simulations of things that do not exist. We like illusions.

3. No drama..... No fun.

Then there is your passion for drama. No film would be complete without drama in some form or another. The action and excitement makes you forget your human form and draws you into another world. Remove all the drama, and instead of thinking say… "what a great story", you might be thinking that the director / producers could have done a better job.

Also notice that you often take pleasure in relating your experiences to other people. Observe the pleasure you get from getting others to relive or fantasise about some experience you have had. We will often call this conversation, but for the most part we are sharing experiences and desires. In the process we get other people to experience our illusions.

What would your life be like if all the excitement were to be removed ?

How dull and boring would that be ?

Just Notice

Just notice your passion for fantasies in whatever form they take.

Then consider if, possibly, on balance, you exhibit any desire to be "different" from what you are ?

How often do you exhibit a desire to experience something other than your present human form ?

This desire to be different is a distorted "echo" of what you really are. Distorted in one crucial way. Both you, and what you think you are right now, enjoy experiencing something different. The real you loves itself with a deep and unconditional passion, while what you think you are has a great difficulty in doing so unconditionally.

As you recognise what you are, so do you recover the ability to love yourself and everyone around you.

Which brings us to one final observation in this section; you wrote the "movie script". To really enjoy the film, you needed to forget that you wrote it. Giving yourself a massive dose of amnesia or memory loss, therefore, makes perfect sense.

However, there is a twist to what you have created. To make the illusion even more exciting, even though you ultimately created the script, to a limited extent you gave "the action" a degree of free will.

You will experience desires to do things. What you ultimately do is not known.

7 Difficult To Control Thoughts And Emotions

Difficult to control thoughts and emotions are one of the most powerful aspects of the illusion you are experiencing. Take a moment to notice how often your mind has been swamped with a particular thought or recurring conversation you cannot get out of your head.

Thinking Patterns

Your thinking easily gets locked into particular patterns. Once the pattern is established, it is difficult to break. One of the most clever aspects of your brain's ability is its automation of high speed calculations. For example, it converts visual impressions of a ball flying through the air into an accurate hand movement that can catch the ball in a split-second. The skill takes years to learn, but then you have it for life. Similarly, the approach you take to thinking has taken years to learn and is now highly automated.

Neural Linguistic Programming is one approach to changing the pattern and hence outcome of your thinking process. You can reprogramme yourself to react differently to situations. However, one fundamental challenge still remains even if you reprogramme your thinking. You still tend to relate to yourself as your thoughts and emotions. To break out of that illusion you have to do more than "shuffle the cards".

Thinking Is Driven By Emotional Energies

Your thinking is driven by your emotional energies or feelings. Your thinking in turn affects your emotional energies or feelings. Of the two, your emotional energies or feelings are the dominant force.

Your thinking helps you connect to new emotional energies or feelings so you can to some extent think yourself into a different state. However, as the emotional energies or feelings are dominant, they easily take you go right back to the emotional state you were previously in. For example, you could feel depressed, and decide to put a smile on your face. You could then feel happier for a while, but the dominant force will tend to remerge later and you will feel depressed again.

This is where many people make a fundamental mistake in the understanding of how to control your emotions. Your thoughts can bury feelings for a while. But these thoughts will tend to resurface later as your thinking does not really control them. Trying to control your emotional energies or feelings with your thoughts actually achieves very little in the long term.

This is one of the reasons why the expression "reverted to type" is used when someone returns to an old behaviour pattern. Even though you can learn new behaviour patterns, you will not easily change the emotional energies or feelings that inspired the old behaviour patterns. So trying to bury your feelings or urges to do something is ultimately a waste of time.

This is essentially why when you find yourself locked in "undesirable" patterns of thoughts and emotions it is very difficult to escape them. You can temporarily distract yourself. But as long as you fail to recognise the illusion you are in, you cannot change them.

Examples of this are so many this book could be filled with them and nothing else, so please understand that the examples listed are only a very small selection:

- Likes or dislikes
- Sexual orientation and desires
- Fear of, flying, failure, conflict, etc, etc.
- Attraction to a person or object.
- Happiness

As you can see, the above list of emotional energies or feelings can easily provide most of the ingredients to create a person's human Earhtly identity.

Changing The Pattern

When you believe you are not experiencing an illusion you will have the most extreme difficulty changing your thoughts and emotions, because you will be living in the illusion that you are your thoughts and emotions.

Many people attempt to solve this by imagining that they are in an illusion, as opposed to noticing it. Thinking you are in an illusion, without actually seeing it being created, is a fantasy, hence that is also an illusion, and you still will have extreme difficulty changing anything. In fact, you have probably just made the challenge even harder.

The number one difficulty you face, in changing the emotional energies or feelings you experience, is your lack of awareness that you really did want to feel them, in the first place. This is not easy to recognise if you are feeling upset, angry or depressed. For in such a state, you will happily argue that such feelings were a mistake and you never wanted to experience them.

Ceasing “the battle” with the thoughts and feelings you experience is an essential step in seeing through the illusion you are experiencing. If you persist with a conflict of this sort you will never be aware enough to see yourself creating your “original problem”.

To retrieve control over your emotional energies or feelings, you need to become aware of yourself at the “level” at which you are creating them. A good indication that your awareness is touching that level is that you recognise how you wanted an “interesting life”. Seeing this with a laugh and a smile is a very good indication that you are succeeding in being more self-aware and change is then easier.

People who are upset about a “problem” are generally not interested in seeing the “funny side”. They instead focus themselves on “seriously” solving their “problem”. Being serious consistently reduces your awareness of how you are creating your “problem”. So you tend not to recognise how you are contributing to the “problem” in the first place.

When you switch to being more aware, you often end up laughing as you recognise that you were complaining about something you were actually creating. At that moment you will be able to change what you are creating and will deal with the “problem” differently and normally far more successfully.

Don’t even bother trying to make yourself laugh if you really do not want to. It does not work. You will only bury the emotions that are causing you trouble.

View From The Astral

Meanwhile, if you felt upset at an Earht level, then from an Astral perspective we would see the "Special Effects Team" hard at work. On the Earht plane you might say "I am upset". At an Astral level you would say "some lower spirit beings are giving me the experience of feeling upset".

When, on the Earht plane, you think, or say, "I am upset", you are correct. You are experiencing being something that is making you feel upset. You are experiencing the product of some lower spirit being. It is they who actually manifest and to a certain extent control your emotions.

The simple reason why you get stuck in difficult-to-control thoughts and emotions is you stop being aware that you wanted to experience them in the first place. Viewed from the Astral, you can start to recognise that this is what you wanted. But on the Earht plane, you can deny this truth by keeping yourself in a low state of awareness. The more you continue to deny this is the experience you wanted, the lower your awareness becomes. Thus with a lower awareness, Free Will and change become even harder.

For example, divorcing couples often have extreme difficulty in finding ways to co-exist, albeit separately. A win-win approach is difficult to adopt when you want the other person to suffer. So agreeing a sensible way forward actually becomes undesirable, and hence very difficult. Even though someone going through a divorce will often claim to want "a happier life", to a large extent that person is working through a desire to make their ex-partner suffer. Denying this truth makes it very difficult to achieve a win-win solution. On the Earht plane, it is very difficult to recognise such behaviour in yourself.

This is where you can benefit directly from this book. By not identifying yourself as a thought and emotion, you give yourself the freedom to be something different and perhaps "smarter". You do not have to control these "difficult" thoughts and emotions. You only need recognise that they are not you. You are the creator and free to choose what you experience. It is merely a matter of increasing your awareness.

8 Everyday Miracle

"The Great Simulator" you are experiencing affects you in so many different ways you rapidly become overwhelmed and start to believe that what you are perceiving yourself to be is your real identity. This illusion, therefore, imposes many limitations upon what you perceive you are capable of. One of the purposes of this book is to enable you to experience more of your natural ability. To release more of your ability, it is important to release you from some profoundly false impressions.

Fundamentally, most people think that they are the same person, more or less, throughout their lifetime. You will remember being a child, you will remember growing up. You will remember doing things you are proud of. You will remember doing things you are less proud of. You will have the strong impression that you have been experiencing a continuous life.

This sense of you living a continuous life is one of the most powerful illusions you are dominated by. It causes you to develop and maintain a completely false sense of identity based upon what you think you were.

Continuously Different Identity

To understand what your false identity really looks like, here is an analogy that has successfully enlightened many people. Remember how a cinema film is composed of many different slides or frames. When these slides are flashed in front of you at 24 frames per second your brain does not register them as completely separate moments, but instead considers them to be a flow of continuous action.

Furthermore, when you watch a film, notice how the scene or camera position is continuously and abruptly changed. Yet your brain will still knit these completely individual slides or frames together and give you the impression of one continuous action sequence.

Take a moment to notice how much the personality you are being changes. You will no doubt have previously experienced being angry and having to control rage. You will also have experienced being very kind, warm and loving. On other occasions you will have experienced being aloof and detached.

To an outside observer, it could easily appear that you were completely different personalities occupying the same physical body. Yet your brain is designed to give you the impression that you are simply one integrated person. Your human brain is designed to give you the impression that the multiple and hugely different personality slides or frames are all you.

However, the greater reality is that you are simply experiencing being a great variety of different personalities.

Typically, under normal conditions, you, the human consciousness, will not recognise what you actually are. Instead you will experience wanting to be "something". Thus, you will tend to identify yourself as whatever you perceive yourself to be. Which is a wide variety of different personalities that all appear to be a unified person. It can be, and usually is, a very convincing illusion of oneness despite the wide variety.

Effect Of Other People

Now, if it were just your own misconception of what is happening, that you had to contend with, you might have some chance of recognising what was happening. However, other people are constantly also perceiving you as being the illusion you were experiencing. This means that not only do you perceive yourself to have a fixed human identity, but the other humans you will experience meeting on Earht will constantly reinforce this deception. Take some simple examples:

1. You and others identify you by name. Say that when you are a happy smiling person they called you "A". If you were a miserable depressed person they do not call you "B", instead they still call you "A". So there is a constant reinforcement that two completely different personalities are not "A" and "B", but just "A".

2. As your physical appearance is more constant, you will still tend to be identified as "A". So every time you or someone else sees your physical body, they will tend to identify you as being "A" and not person "B", "C", "D", etc. Even though you might not be manifesting the personality of "A", but instead being "B", "C", or "D", etc.

3. Then there is the matter of ownership. Everyone experiencing "The Great Simulator" will appear to own something:

   His house.
   Her car.
   His shirt.
   Her necklace.

All these impressions and conventions reinforce the idea that you are one unified being with memories of having experienced various things. In fact, you are just experiencing being multiple personalities in different situations. None of them are you, yet "good" or "bad", you and other people will tend to identify you as being all of them. As this process starts from birth, and most people know nothing else, the absence of contrast with experiencing your real self make the illusion highly convincing.

This section is called an "Everyday Miracle". The miracle is that every morning you wake up and, even though you will be experiencing being a new and unique personality, you will tend to think that you are the sum of all the previous ones.

Use Your Ability To Change

If you are still not sure what I am helping you recognise, then consider the following two alternatives:

- How many people, you included, awake every morning to recognise that it is another day in which you can enjoy being something new, exciting and different ?

Or…..

- How many people, including you, awaken thinking that they are the "same old person" who has to solve "yesterday's problems" ?

Because you tend to identify yourself as what you previously were, you are less open to the potential of what you could be.

One of the purposes of this book is to help you experience and enjoy many more of your potential abilities. This objective is made much easier when you recognise that you are NOT something that has already "ceased to exist" like a slide, or frame on a film, now past and never to return.

Effect Of Perception

A demonstration I often enjoy doing with people is to get them to experience actually being stronger or weaker depending on how I relate to them. Even when these clients know that I am doing the demonstration on them, the simple power of verbal suggestion is enough to influence their actual physical strength.

For added entertainment, the demonstration still works even if I say nothing to them. I simply look into their eyes and when I perceive them as stronger, they get physically stronger. Similarly, when I perceive them as weaker, even though I have said nothing, they get weaker.

If I were to spend time with you and take you through this demonstration you would recognise how much your perception of yourself if influenced by other people, even when nothing is actually said. The effect is so strong it affects your physical abilities.

This effect works because, ultimately, there is only one of us and emotional energies permeate all human consciousnesses.

Another example of this in action can be seen when two people have developed a strong negative impression of each other. A divorcing couple are often experts in this respect. One of the partners will often find that they get inexplicably unreasonable when dealing with the other one. This tends to happen because the other one sees the first as unreasonable and the perception becomes a reality. This happens even when the first partner is making a conscious effort to be "nice" to the second partner.

You are migrating from one identity to another. The everyday miracle is that you will tend to believe that they are all you. After reading this, that will happen less often.

9 Birth & Death

The Astral World is your real home and allows you to experience "The Great Simulator". The Earht plane or dimension is just an aspect of a sub-world that you "visit". From many perspectives the Earht plane appears not to exist at all, as the illusion it really is makes attributing "solidity" to it appear a completely ridiculous notion.

Depending on where you are focused in the Astral World you may or may not appear to be an individual. In simplistic terms as you go "lower" in the Astral World you will appear to be an individual. Therefore at the lower levels, instead of it being quite obvious that there is really only one of us, there now appears to be many of us. It is really very amusing to recognise this when you see the "joke of it all".

Living as a human being allows you to experience virtually the complete opposite of what you really are. As mentioned earlier in this book, there are "echoes" of what you really are and these help you recognise your true self. As a human consciousness you will tend not to recognise most of these "echoes" of your true identity, and instead you will remain focused on your Earthly form.

In the Astral World you appear to be a consciousness which is a sort of cloud of energy. The lower you go, the more human attributes your consciousness acquires or, more accurately, borrows. As you get closer to the Earht plane you appear to be a consciousness with a full package of human personalities and forms. In effect you look like all the things you plan to be on Earht simultaneously:

- Foetus
- Baby
- Toddler
- Child
- Etc
- Etc
- Pensioner
- Pensioner about to die

Conversely, when your human form dies, your consciousness refocuses "higher up" in the Astral World and you shed or lose most of the human attributes you had previously borrowed.

In practice you do not really move anywhere in the Astral World, it would be more accurate to say that you appear to focus yourself in different areas of it. Though you don't actually move anywhere when you do this, you instead have the impression that you have moved around in the Astral World by apparently refocusing yourself.

Getting Born

When you are born onto the Earht plane, from an Astral World perspective it looks like you are consumed by a cloud of Earhtly impressions. Your guiding spirits would be right there with you, but you would be under the strong impression that you were alive on Earth and probably alone. When your physical body dies and the human impressions fall away, your guiding spirits are there to greet you, even though you have not really gone anywhere.

It is, of course possible to see right through this illusion and recognise that your guiding spirits are right there with you. But to achieve this you have to address the fact that you wanted to experience a human life and experience this illusion. This CAN NOT be done merely by thinking that you want the illusion to stop. The thoughts you would be having are only a consequence of the illusion and therefore in no position to determine if the illusion should stop.

From the "lower" Astral World perspective, you might say that getting born looks like someone climbing into a "bubble of energy". To the human consciousness it appears to be more like getting sucked down a funnel. Once sucked in you experience a severe loss of awareness and strong amnesia or memory loss. Ironically, the loss of awareness is so strong that you forget that you have forgotten what you really are. Your human form starts to appear to be all you are.

Going Home

On the "way out" at your physical death, naturally the reverse applies. You get the impression of something like travelling back up a tunnel of light and you "step out of the bubble". It is easy and straight forward.

Death, does however, often come with one temporary complication. During the transition between thinking you are a human being and remembering that you never were, you can be inclined to retain elements of your human identity. In some cases this causes you to remain close to the Earht plane as a ghost, for a while anyway. But eventually you will get "rescued" either by your guiding spirits, or a human being on the Earht plane who recognises what has happened and helps you on your way.

Another confusion, is not recognising that you have died. Your experience immediately at death is designed to be a combination of what you expect combined with a re-orientation to help you recognise what you really are and where you were. This is normally an individual experience and governed by how quickly you recognise that you are "returning to normal". However, the matter is complicated if you are resistant to the fact that whilst your physical body may be dead, you are not. Because you perceive yourself to be alive, which you are, you can have difficulty accepting that this is possible without a physical body. Human consciousnesses in this condition are very confused and resistant to "reason", so they can get stuck for years, but as they are also largely oblivious of Earhtly time this is not a problem. They always get "collected" in the end.

I can personally recall a previous incarnation memory of just such a confusion. It was 1945 during the battle of Berlin. That human consciousness experienced death as a result of getting machine-gunned. Four bullets struck diagonally from shoulder to stomach. Death resulted, but the human consciousness was naturally very much alive. I can still recall the confusion that arose from experiencing a fatal wounding, but feeling alive. I then recall making sense of this with the thought that perhaps sub-machinegun wounds were not fatal, whilst rifle ones were. Fortunately I, and as I now recall, a number of other deceased, were rounded up by a Guide posing as a military office. It was off to heaven for us.

When you die, you generally experience yourself getting separated from your body and can end up in "strange places". If you are confused, look out for deceased relatives or friends. They are there to help you discard your human form and "ascend" into the light. Even a deceased family pet can be there to greet you. I often tell my soon to be deceased (2007) father; "If you find yourself walking the dog, you are dead". At the time of writing this is a fair comment as our deceased dog (appearing as a spirit) is sitting beside my father's bed waiting to take him for a walk. In the later versions of this series of books I will be in a position to tell you what happened.

It is also normal, and where appropriate or possible, to attend your own funeral. Seeing people mourning your dead human body helps you recognise what has happened, which is useful as you will be feeling "very much alive". In the absence of your old body which may have got lost (e.g. Blown to pieces in an explosion), a memorial service will usually help. It also helps those left on the Earht plane to "let go"; if they do not, you will experience a curious pull as they try to draw you back.

Reading these words, for example, will cause you to try to imagine what death is like. However, what you imagine will never turn out to be the way it is. So stay relaxed, open-minded and you will be looked after.

Most consciousnesses who have exited "The Great Simulator's" Earht plane tend to "rest" for a while which allows you to dispense with many of the illusions of human identity you were experiencing. If you don't "rest", you tend to find yourself rapidly back on the Earht plane having a continuation of your last human experience.

Most consciousnesses have experienced the Earht plane before and will do so again. This is the subject of reincarnation and is covered next.

10 Reincarnation

Confusing

Some people have recognised that you can "live again". Some people have recognised that "you do not live again". Both groups are correct and incorrect.

Personally, to begin with I went along with the "you live again on Earht " group. However, as the years and practical experience of the subject developed, it became clear that the matter was far from clear-cut. I used to think that we had a linear progression of one life to another. There is evidence for this and you can experience it for yourself. In fact, I recommend you do so, as it is highly enlightening.

Though, as time went on, various anomalies surfaced. For one thing, the simple linear model, of one life followed by another, was confused by the observation that you could be starting a new life before you had finished the last one.

It also became apparent, that I appeared to be (like you too are) at least one guiding spirit in the Astral World. For example, a clairvoyant client said that I would sometimes visit her and radiate healing energies (blue in this case). Now I, the human, had no conscious memory of this, but as there were other independent sightings of me, in the Guide role, the manifestation had to be acknowledged.

Hence, it was around this time that I became aware that both myself, and other people, had what might best be described as "guiding spirit past lives". It became clear that instead of only having just the memories of being various humans alive on Earht, you can also recall memories of being guiding spirits helping humans on Earht. Each memory produces a combination of both "watching a film", whilst also "experiencing being in that film".

This is where the linear model of one lifetime following another really breaks down. As you are probably now aware, a guiding spirit can be in two places at once. The direct consequence of which is that you, the human being, can possess overlapping previous incarnation memories.

The basic challenge in translating your Earhtly experience of what you tend to think are, into the reality of the situation, is that you are very attached to your human identity. This human identity dictates that you are separate from other humans, guides and everything else. However, a human consciousness, the thing you will tend to believe you are, is made from multiple components. Furthermore, the God / super-consciousness, hence soul component, has no real personality / human identity, and exists everywhere. So the true essence of what you are is actually living every life, be it human, animal, vegetable, mineral or alien. Your independent human identity is but a powerful and compelling illusion.

For this "simple" technical reason, the components that comprise your human consciousness can easily be in two places at once. So the Guides that organise your personality are actually having multiple experiences in different bodies simultaneously.

If you said that the human consciousness was formed from say, 10 guiding spirits (these are not actual figures) working together, then you would not be too far from the truth. Then you could also recognise that say 4 of those guiding spirits were also helping create another life with a different 6 other guiding spirits elsewhere. Multiple existences are suddenly possible.

In very simplistic terms here is what appears to be happening:

1. You, the super-consciousness, want to create a human experience. You manifest your intention through what we can describe as a “soul”.

2. A soul has no personality. So to create one, guiding spirits assemble themselves around that soul to create human consciousnesses. By this method you, the human consciousness, then appear to exist.

However, the mix of what you are not only changes from one life to another, but during that life. Additionally, parts of what creates you will be simultaneously creating other human lives, many times, and this is without even considering the contribution of the lower spirit forms.

If this is your first experience of this subject, I hope you are confused, it’s a sign that you are waking up.

The linear “Reincarnation Model” will not explain everything that you will find. Yet you can recover memories of previous existences that do appear to have some impact on the current one. This is because the Guides that comprise you often work to produce what will appear to be one lifetime after another. Hence, there will often appear to be a steady progression of one incarnation after another.

Multiple incarnations are like having one life lesson after another. This means that an accumulation of skill and ability will appear to occur. People who appear to have worked on a subject such as “art” over many lifetimes will appear more and more instantly gifted upon each reincarnation. Then, just to confuse everyone, they will switch off most of that ability, in subsequent lifetimes, as the mix of Guides changes.

You will also find that the reincarnation "memories" you carry can contain memories of repeating similar experiences several times. Sometimes, instead of containing skills, these memories appear to possess fears and blockages, which you will be trying to resolve in this lifetime.

If you think that this collection of skills and problems is limited to your previous Earht experiences, then there is one last factor to consider. The Astral World comprises a great many realms or other worlds. If you ever wondered what life could be like on other planets, you don't need a space ship to find out; just take a look at your previous experiences.

In summary:

- Most human consciousness will have some "memory" of previous incarnations.

- These memories contain both abilities and apparent blockages.

- Because, to some extent, the team of Guides keeps altering, it is inaccurate to suggest that you are the same person during one lifetime, let alone over many incarnations.

- Plus there are the parallel and overlapping incarnations to consider……

OBSERVATION

If you can relate to the idea that you, the human consciousness, are simply a collection of Guides experiencing human existence, then everything starts to make "more sense". As each of the component Guides will have had a variety of previous human experiences, you, the human consciousness, will have memories buried within you of those various previous existences. They will not be "linear", but they will affect your current human identity.

How To Access Previous Incarnations

There are basically two approaches to recovering memories of previous incarnations.

METHOD 1

Get hypnotised. Once your brain has stopped worrying about life and gone quiet under a deep relaxation, the hypnotist can start having a "look around". This works on lots of people and you can find a great many books on the subject. The disadvantage is that you often do not remember what you saw and re-experienced whilst under hypnosis.

METHOD 2

Astral Projection. Often this can require little more than sitting quietly. Once your brain has stopped trying to "solve things" you have immediate access to the Astral World. People make the mistake of trying really hard to do this and that will not help you project. Anyway, the memories of previous incarnations are literally all around you. Ultimately, the challenge is not connecting to them, but making sense of them.

Effects Of Previous Incarnations

This difficult-to-comprehend tangle does have a simple effect you can observe. Most people who try, can recollect previous and even future incarnations. Each life is unique, which is why the "one life" group are correct, but lives are inter-connected, which is why the "more than one life" group are also correct.

Overall, experiences of other lives will tend to have some impact upon the one you are experiencing right now. If hypnotised, most people will have memories of something, but until you can go beyond your desire to experience an independent human identity, you will never comprehend what is happening. And that's the way you wanted it to be (Part 2 will give you a more comprehensive understanding of this).

The memories of previous incarnations are stored in the Astral World. All methods of recovering these memories require consciously accessing the Astral World. Ultimately, the only way to have an intelligent conversation with anyone, on this subject, is for you to both become consciously aware of the Astral World at the same time and compare notes. Otherwise one, or both of you, will be imagining it, and that puts you straight back into the Earht plane illusion. So until you are consciously accessing the Astral World for yourself, it is pointless for you to try and work out the precise truth behind reincarnation. In the meantime, just become aware that this influence exists, and that it is most probably affecting you.

Most people have these memories and they do influence your current behaviour and abilities. In my work with clients I found endless examples of previous behaviour and experiences impacting on the present. Here are some examples:

- A relationship between a man and a woman where the man had a latent inclination to kill the woman. In their last incarnation together, he succeeded. This time round, he is trying not to and she is trying to make sure he does not. They were both still alive the last time I enquired.

- A female client, who had a fear of drowning, turned out to have previously been a sailor who was thrown overboard tied to a heavy rock. Remembering the drowning experience helped reduce the otherwise inexplicable fear.

- A male client who has strong memories of how to be a "Spiritual Master". In this case, the memory acts as a useful reminder of what is possible. It is also an inspiration to recreate something similar but in the more challenging environment of a 21st century city.

Normally, for behaviour patterns, fears and skills, from a previous lifetime to manifest in this one, some form of recreation must take place. Typically, you will recreate a situation so as to have a second chance to handle it differently. It is worth noting that while there is no actual "right" or "wrong" outcome you have to achieve, many possibilities, normally, exist.

Do You Need To Check Your Previous Incarnations

No, is the simple general answer. To be a little more accurate, if you need to you will and, if you don't, you won't. In your normal human state you will not be experiencing much Free Will. As a consequence of that, you don't have a great deal of freedom to decide what you will, or will not, do. If it supports your "life path" to remember your previous incarnations, then you will. You will not normally be in a position to make a truly conscious decision to do so or not. If you need to, you will.

Most of the experiences of relevance to us from our previous incarnations concern relationships with other people. You will tend to find that situations often get repeated. Discovering that you have been in the same "ridiculous" situation before often brings a new impetus to act differently in the present.

Investigating your previous incarnations normally reveals a wealth of interesting memories and experiences, not all of them pleasant. The first memory I consciously recovered was of a violent death resulting from a sword, or similar heavy object, smashing into my head. It took me approximately six months to get over the worst of the re-experience. Furthermore, I now still feel frightened when objects travel towards my head at high speed.

However, most memories are more mundane and less troubling. Many are interesting and amusing, but try not to get stuck trying to relive a previous incarnation when you can be enjoying the adventure of this one.

11 Practical Problem Solving

Right now I am going to explain some simple principles of something that has the potential to change your life. However, even though you will intellectually understand them, that will not be enough. You will need to follow the practical exercises in Part 2 of this book to benefit fully. You both need to understand intellectually and then apply practically if you are to succeed.

This section is devoted to mapping out the road that lies ahead of you. Later we will walk down it together.

Fundamental Observation No1

You have abundant energy and enthusiasm to do the things you want to do. When you want to do something you experience a high level of creativity and inventiveness that enables you to succeed.

When you do not want to do something, you will block that same enthusiasm and creativity. Once you block your ability to operate at your full potential you are now in a position to easily fail and under-perform.

You cannot make yourself want to do something you do not want to do.

You can, however, resolve why you did not want to do it, and hence discover why you actually do want to do it with energy and enthusiasm, or you will discover there is a great alternative you want to achieve instead.

When you do not appear capable of doing something, it is very likely that you don't want to do it; so stop trying to fool yourself.

Fundamental Observation No2

You already know the answers to most of the challenges you face at this moment.

I have consistently found that people generally knew exactly what they needed to do next. Yet these same people had, for whatever reason, decided that they were somehow incapable of doing what needed to be done.

It's all down to the perfect but limited functioning of your brain. Your brain calculates whether or not you appear capable of doing something. Say for example, jumping over a wall. If you are fully energised, your brain will do the calculation and tell you….. GO. But if you do not want to do it (see Fundamental Observation No1) you will feel apathetic. Your brain will do the same calculation based on your enthusiasm and tell you……. DON'T DO IT.

Much as your brain helps you fantasise about the past and the future, it only actually operates in the "now". So it will base all action calculations on what you perceive yourself to be, in that moment.

Even if you know how to do something, your brain will tell you that "jumping over the wall" is not an option, if you feel sluggish and de-energised. It does not want you to get hurt, so it will tell you that "jumping over the wall" is not an option. It will start looking for different options. Do you see the illusion ?

Conclusion

We spend a great deal of time talking nonsense, or put more crudely "rubbish", to ourselves. Now there are some parts of this book that can be initially difficult to check for yourself, such as the reality of the Astral World. However, this section has immediate and easy-to-spot benefits when you are looking.

Believing our own "rubbish" helps to create the illusion of human existence you are experiencing. The more you recognise that you are regularly talking "rubbish" to yourself, the easier it is to recognise the reality of what is actually happening.

Insight

People spend a great amount of time pretending to try and solve problems and challenges. Furthermore, they claim they do not want to have to resolve these problems or challenges.

Note that you frequently do this.

However, you also have the potential to react differently. When it comes to solving practical problems you basically have two options:

OPTION 1: Complain and de-energise.

OPTION 2: Recognise why you have created this challenge and energise yourself into action.

You do not always have to solve the initial problem; there are often alternatives. But ultimately you do need to recognise why you were creating it. If you don't, it will re-emerge in a new form again and again.

People complain they have problems or challenges to solve. Because we tend to talk "rubbish" to ourselves we do not easily notice how we actually created those problems or challenges in the first place.

Change your approach to resolving problems and challenges, and your whole life will change.

Free Will & Problem Solving

You will generally not experience much Free Will when it comes to problem solving because it was your Free Will that probably created the "problem" in the first place.

Having to sort out "problems" can make human beings highly energised. Solving problems and challenges is a highly creative and enjoyable activity. Puzzles are a classic example.

Alternatively, having to sort out "problems" can lead to making human beings upset. When you are upset you will be experiencing a low level of awareness. At these low levels you have very little access to your Free Will.

People often make the mistake of thinking that Free Will is a thought. Whereas, it would be more accurate to describe Free Will as an Energy that causes thoughts. Hence, thoughts are not a very efficient method of directing your Free Will.

In Part 2 we are going to look at practical approaches to converting irritation at having to "solve problems" into a force that “solves them”, even though the solution may not always be what you expected.

To help you attain an attitude that will support “problem solving”, there is a very helpful first step you can make. Keep noticing how you can choose your reaction to challenges.

When a “problem” arises you do not have to get annoyed. You could have a wide range of reactions. Recognise that you can start to access your Free Will by choosing your reactions to situations.

Time Saving Tip

A common mistake is to try to be “happy” when you are feeling very “upset”. If something upsets or annoys you, that feeling is the result of an energy or force for change. If you just try to block it out by being “happy”, you block the force for change.

Practice converting the “upset” feeling and its driving energy into something more positive and useful. Then you will be accessing a new creative energy that will help you resolve your original “problem”. This is your path to accessing your Free Will.

12 The Great Simulator

We are now coming to the end of Part 1. In Part 2 we are going to practice some practical exercises that make it much easier for you to fundamentally change the way in which you experience this life. Similarly if you want to make changes, you will find it easier to exercise your Free Will and create those changes.

But before we move forward, let us summarise the amazing illusion you are experiencing:

- You will have a persistent sense of identity that repeatedly convinces you that you are a living breathing human being alive on Earth.

- You will tend to have a poor awareness of what you really are because you are wilfully, but largely unconsciously, blocking it out.

- You block your awareness by constantly imagining things and having conversations in your head.

- You will be experiencing a large degree of distracting thoughts and emotions that “keep you busy”.

- Everyone else appears very separate, even though there is really only one of us.

- It is very difficult to recognise that you actually wanted every problem or challenge you face.

- Your sense of fun and unconditional love will often appear to be absent.

- It will often appear ridiculous that it is your Free Will which has created all the "problems" you face.

Test This For Yourself

You may not believe a single word of what I have written for you. I do, however, most strongly suggest that you test everything for yourself. There is not much point in reading this and trying to imagine what is meant. Similarly if you try to work it out or rationalise these things you will ultimately fail. You need to learn how to be significantly more self-aware. The simple fact of the matter is that because your imagination and rationalisation is a significant part of how the illusion is created in the first place, using it to break out is futile. It's like trying to put out a fire by throwing petrol on it.

When you become more self-aware you will notice the following:

- You are frequently self-sabotaging yourself. Then believing the illusion that you are less capable then you really are.

- Upset emotions will either paralyse you or energise you into action. You should notice when you are paralysing yourself or making good use of them.

- You take yourself seriously. Your attachment to your human identity prevents you from resolving many of the challenges you face.

See The world As It Really Is

This book was written to help you recognise that the solid world around you is not what is appears to be. When you see it for what it really is, you will find it so amusing that you just have to laugh. Sometimes the experience of recognising the truth makes you smile so much it becomes painful. When you connect to your unconditional love you will often want to cry. You cannot imagine or rationalise these experiences, you can only experience them.

People who have learnt to see that they are actively creating their own Earhtly experience typically enjoy the following benefits.

- You will feel happier, and able to enjoy your life to a far greater extent.
- You will find that because you are much more alert to the guidance of your natural intuition (Guides); you now make much better decisions.
- You will be more successful at what you do, or change what you do and be more successful at your new venture.

Learn To Break Out Of Everyday Illusions

Cynical people might say that this book is telling you to ignore the Earhtly illusion around you and relax into a docile, unproductive life as everything will ultimately be ok.

WRONG...... This book is here to help you recognise that:

1. You are experiencing this amazing illusion because you wanted to, therefore ignoring it is not helpful.

2. The book is to help you live….. not escape.

The exercises in Part 2 will enable you to break out of a variety of illusions. Many of the people I have already helped were trapped in a false perception of themselves. Here are some examples of some of their self-perceptions:

- I am the person who has "X" problem to solve.
- I am not good enough.
- I would be better if…………..
- I never had the chance to…………
- I am held back by………..
- I can't be happy until………..

Thinking this "rubbish" is something you wanted to do to make the illusion real. It makes you take yourself seriously. In fact thinking this "rubbish" turns out to be a very amusing part of what you are experiencing. You will laugh and cry with unconditional love whenever you allow yourself to see the truth.

Living With More Self Awareness

The next part of this book focuses on simple exercises that when implemented will make a significant difference to your life. Sometimes, people suggest it is a dramatic transition from which you can never go back. Well, that will turn out to be at least half true.

The extraordinary fact is that even though you will see the illusion happening one minute, you can forget everything and start taking yourself seriously the next.

Experience has shown that clients can move from being incredibly insightful and capable one minute, then demonstrate a complete lack of awareness the next, and then go back to being insightful and highly capable.

You could say that following a "higher awareness" approach you can spend more time being "smarter" and less time being "stupid". However, I have yet to see anyone (including myself) eliminate the "stupid" moments. This is because ultimately we are having a great deal of fun being "stupid". In many ways "stupid" is more amusing that "smart".

What makes someone who has developed their self-awareness different is that that person can consciously decide when they want to stop being "stupid" and revert to "smart", which is actually your natural condition. You no longer get locked in the identity of someone you do not like.

The fact that you are reading this book is clear evidence that at some level you intend to recognise that you are in The Great Simulator. By following the practical exercises in the next part you will gain deep insights into how The Great Simulator functions. People normally have extreme difficulty in changing their lives. The Great Simulator is a machine you need to understand if you want to be in a position to easily make changes that will benefit you.

What are the things you want to change ?

Overview Of The Great Simulator

In this book I don't want to just give you my impression of the purpose of The Great Simulator. If I did, and you did not test the information for yourself, then you would not really know for yourself.

Understanding the purpose of The Great Simulator cannot be done merely by imagining what these words might mean. You have to "see" it for yourself. Therefore please understand that the overview is a simplified "road map" to help you get there. It is not a precise description. You need to discover the precise details for yourself.

Summary of the simulator structure

The Great Simulator is formed from what is often called the Astral World. It is constructed from an Energy supplied by one Super-Consciousness otherwise known as God. In your human form you can experience this Energy as a wonderful Divine Love.

In the high vibration or energy level of the Astral World you can get a sense of what is really happening. That region of the Astral is formless and there is no noticeable separation. At that level you are aware that there is actually only one of us but, in order to create The Great Simulator, it is necessary to give the impression of many overlapping entities.

As you descend the energy levels you can see the separation starting to manifest. The separated bits of the super-consciousness, or God, are now reformed to create individual consciousnesses. At this level you start to find Angelic beings and if you go a little lower, Guides. However, it would be unfair to see the two groups as that different. Let's call them the Higher Beings.

As you go lower still you find entities that manifest a higher degree of separation. These could be described as Low Vibration Consciousnesses and Elemental Beings. Their variety and multitude renders this description an over-simplification, but let us call them Lower Beings for ease of analysis.

These Lower Beings form the Lower Astral Sub or Mini Worlds. The types of worlds formed are governed by the Higher Beings, who encourage the Lower Beings with an unconditional love energy form. Some of these Sub or Mini Worlds are our human Heavens. Heavens (plural), because there are multiple versions of it.

The whole thing looks like a divine experiment initiated by the super-consciousness or God. Whilst there is a strong intention as to what will happen in The Great Simulator, because it is operated through entities created to manifest independence of sorts, the result is a little unpredictable. Everything is guided, but the details of the outcomes are not predetermined.

The "lower you go", the stronger the illusion of independent conscious life gets.

At the bottom, more or less, come worlds such as our physical universe and hence Earth. Depending upon where you are in The Great Simulator, our universe and Earth can look enormous or extremely small. It can be confusing to begin with.

Then there are the life forms such as animals and humans. Animal consciousnesses are essentially similar to human consciousnesses, except that you would need a few (typically three) animals to make one human. Incidentally there are some other life forms that require a few human consciousnesses to construct.

Human consciousnesses are created from Lower Beings guided and energised by Higher Beings. Not one single human being actually exists, nor does the Earht they think they live on. The Great Simulator instead creates the impression or illusion that they do exist.

At this very moment you will have the impression that you are an independent entity. You are, in fact, imagining this. Because you rarely (if ever) see how you are creating that identity you have very little control over what it does, hence you have virtually no Free Will.

This is the "tough" part for a human consciousness to comprehend. Your life appears so real and well defined. Yet it is a machine that normally has little access to the Free Will that created it. You are not a human-consciousness machine, you are a divine, experiencing something fascinating and often highly amusing. It is always possible to recognise this whenever the machine stops taking itself too seriously and instead loves itself more.

This book is a message from you, to you on the Earht plane. It is intended to help you to "wake up". In the course of "waking up" you start to recognise what you are and actually manifest some Free Will.

Your Next Step

Imagining you are in an illusion you are already imagining changes nothing. You have to make a fundamental shift in your awareness and, hence, human capability.

Following the exercises in Part 2 will help you step through the illusion and recognise what you are creating. That gives you access to your Free Will.

The awareness exercises that follow are based on advanced training techniques that have been practiced for thousands of years. As you are reading this book, the likelihood is that you have previous incarnation connections in which you have already done the ground work for your next step.

Accessing your Free Will revolutionises your human existence.

Do these exercises properly and you will discover this for yourself.

Have fun.

David

The Great Simulator

But You Wanted To Believe You Were

Part 2

Introduction To Part 2

In Part 1 we looked into the basic design of The Great Simulator.

In Part 2 we will explore how you actually see The Great Simulator in action.

Learning to see The Great Simulator in action is a bit like "waking up" from a compelling dream. It is a gradual process that takes practice. "Waking up" is both a Science, and an Art. The techniques that enable you to do so are relatively simple, however, the practice will not be that easy.

The basic challenge you face in "waking up" is that you wanted to be "asleep" in the first place. This is a powerful force that you CAN NEVER overcome; it is stronger than a human consciousness and, ultimately, was put there by you.

Fortunately, the design of The Great Simulator permits you to "wake up" if you develop your awareness. As you develop your awareness you will gradually give yourself permission to "wake up" and the force that previously kept you "asleep" will progressively diminish. Ultimately you do not have to overcome the force that puts you to "sleep", instead, its influence diminishes as you become more self-aware.

As I said, "waking up" is both a Science and an Art.

The "Science" is a technical understanding of what you are doing. For this reason alone, you require an in-depth comprehension of what you are experiencing, and how it is created. Consequently, you to need understand this from a wide variety of perspectives. At times you may find Part 2 appears to be a little repetitive. However, it is actually giving you new insights from different perspectives.

With respect to the "Art", you only become proficient at being able to see The Great Simulator in action, by practicing, frequently. A painter who creates great masterpieces is basically only applying paint onto canvas. The art of creating a masterpiece is to apply that paint with great skill. Acquiring that skill is only possible through considerable repetition. Similarly, to enable you to acquire the skill and ability to see The Great Simulator in action, you will be given appropriate exercises to follow. Each one builds upon the last, and you will discover that through simple repetition of ever more complex exercises, you will become a Master.

Initially, the exercises in this book are demanding of your concentration. It is like learning to walk, which typically would take a baby approximately one year of repetitive practice. The exercises you will be practicing teach you to "walk through life" in a new way which presents you with many practical benefits.

I hope you enjoy Part 2

David

13 Demystifying The Super-Consciousness

Mysteries cause the truth to be hidden. This book does not claim to know the truth. This book is just an observation of how the world actually appears to be. Observations are something you can also make for yourself, and that gives us some scope for potential agreement.

If we were instead to remain committed to maintaining a massive mystery, then we are going to have lots of scope for disagreement. Disagreement can develop into violence, fatwa's, and lots of upset feelings. This book is simply here to give you some practical techniques to enable you to gain a new understanding of what you really are, and what you are experiencing as a human being. To that end it is the clear intention of this book to eliminate as many mysteries as possible.

Whether you choose to use the term God or Super-Consciousness, ultimately does not matter. To save me some typing, for the moment I will use the term God.

The Way It Appears

For simplicity, you could divide the human race into approximately two groups:

- The ones who experience God as part of their daily lives. (Group 1)

- The ones who don't. (Group 2)

Most people reading this book will fall into the Group 2 category. If you live in a developed country, most of the people you will know will fall into the Group 2 category. Most religious people similarly fall into the Group 2 category.

Let me explain what is happening.

People Who Experience God As Part Of Their Daily Lives (Group 1)

If you live or travel to parts of what is currently known as the "Developing World", you will easily find these sorts of people. They predominantly live in rural communities as opposed to urban ones. They will generally have had little education.

You can recognise them because they tend to look happy.

They are often poor and live with minimal material goods, yet they appear somehow content. It's as if they have connected to a simple joy of being alive.

These people all recognise that they were somehow created by God. The world they live in was created by God. They have a belief that the course of their lives is ultimately dictated by God. Similarly, they tend to have a harmony or sorts with nature and their surroundings.

The existence of God is not questioned by them because they are experiencing it in a "matter of fact way". These people feel God in themselves and the land they work. It is so matter of fact for them that to question the existence of God would be ridiculous.

These people are not biologically different from other human beings; they just relate to the world differently. This is possible because they have not developed their intellectual capacity in the same way that human beings in more urban surroundings have.

You could say that they are having fewer thoughts which block out their sense of God. That is why for such people God is an everyday reality.

The Ones Who Don't (Group 2)

The fact that you are reading this book gives you approximately a 99.9% certainty that you are in this second group.

I would currently place myself in this group.

It's not that you don't experience God from time to time. It is however, the case that you forget about God………… regularly.

Doing so is not a crime, a sin, a mistake, an error, etc, etc. It was the plan. That is what you wanted to happen.

You forget about God because you stop consciously experiencing God. God gets divorced from your "reality". This makes it possible for you to feel that you definitely exist, whilst there may or may not be a God out there somewhere. The degree to which this occurs varies for person to person. Some people will appear to have forgotten altogether, whilst others make a conscious effort to busy themselves trying to remember.

Churches and Temples are built and operated by people who occupy themselves trying to remember. If you are a Group 1 person, you will not have a great deal of need for a church or a temple as you will remember what you are most of the time. Group 1 people often forgo erecting any sort of structure and instead tend to set aside a piece of ground where they go to sharpen their remembering skills. So if it had not been for the Group 2's, the Earht would be devoid of the magnificent temples, cathedrals and similar places of worship it has today.

What both groups 1 and 2 tend to have in common, is that they see God as somehow greater than themselves. In that God has managed to create you and "the universe" there is some basis for this position.

Yet, this overlooks one fact, you are God.

Group 3

Group 1's don't do much thinking about this and tend to see themselves as less than God. Whilst the Group 2's, who mostly recognise that there is a God (somewhere) still tend to think about themselves as less than God.

Your divine plan appears to involve combining the attributes of these two groups into one. This combination creates a thinking human being that recognises God in an everyday way. Experiencing this would mean recognising that you were an aspect of God living in your own amazing creation "The Great Simulator". This is something that Group 1 and 2 human beings have trouble achieving.

In various different forms this has already been achieved by people you might categorise as prophets. But prophets are, on the whole, in 2007, exceptional rather than commonplace. Hence, you could say there are very few Group 3's to be found at the time of writing this book.

One indication of experiencing more of a Group 3 existence would be that you sense a wonderful unconditional love most of the time. You would feel the energy of the super consciousness or God flowing through your physical manifestation. You would recognise and feel this same energy in everything around you. But, most important of all, you would recognise that you were an aspect of God rather than something "less".

Common Misconceptions

It would be inaccurate to call a misconception a mistake. After all, what would be the point of creating The Great Simulator if you did not generate a wealth of wonderful misconceptions. So be clear, the following list of misconceptions are meant to occur in some form or other.

Divine Inspiration

The human consciousness's relationship to God is an interesting one. God has set it up so that a human being will feel desires to behave in various ways. Sometimes they will feel happy, sometimes depressed, etc. Being for the most part "asleep", the human consciousness will not be aware of these forces and will, instead, occupy itself with self-justification. Similarly, you (God) created a situation where you could "see" your magnificence from the perspective of a human being. So it should be no surprise that human beings have a desire to perceive God as somehow greater than themselves. Even though, from a different perspective, that looks like a very amusing practical joke you are playing on yourself.

Everything a human being experiences is the consequence of divine intention. If you feel energised to do a wonderful act of charity, you will justify your actions and do it. You are essentially responding to the energy you experience.

Conversely, you could experience an energy that would start a war where millions of people will die. Again, you will tend to justify your actions and off you would go to war. The driving intention, combined with the human mind's ability to justify anything, make almost any category of human action easily achievable.

You (God) actually energise your human consciousness to want to do various things whilst you "watch" to see if your human consciousness notices what is going on. If a human consciousness is "asleep", it will always follow the intention you gave it. If it is "awake", you will recognise what you are creating for yourself.

As soon as a human consciousness occupies itself with self-justification it goes to "sleep". Sleep, in this instance, means that it will not be self-aware. So your human form can talk and walk, drive cars and perform a wide variety of functions whilst still asleep and barely self-aware.

The human consciousness is subjected to continual divine inspiration, yet it generally fails to notice any of it. The misconception here is that the human consciousness will tend to think it functions independently. If the divine inspiration were to suddenly end, so would the human body that was receiving it. There would be an instantaneous death of that human form.

God Ordered Me To.........

From time to time an Angelic being will manifest itself on Earht and instruct a human being with a few suggestions. This happens quite often. Not all human beings will see these manifestations even when they happen. So a manifestation could, for example, happen to half the people in a room.

If this were the only form of divine intervention life would be simple but, to make it more interesting, there are lots of other manifestations that might "order you around". So as a general principle to guide you, God does not order you around. After all, why would something that has created you, plus inspired and largely defined your desires and actions, need to order you to do anything ?

There are various religious testaments that suggest that God did indeed give various orders. However, take note that these testaments were written a long time ago and have since been translated, often many times, so the likelihood of contextual errors is high.

Your guiding spirits, for example, do not tend to order you around. They will seek to enlighten you by elevating your awareness and making helpful suggestions. Ordering you around would be counter productive to the greater goal of getting human consciousnesses to manifest some Free Will. The closest they normally get to ordering you around is, for example, occasionally, warning you that the course of action you are taking is "stupid" and you will be sorry if you continue.

However, God has created a multitude of spirit forms that will try to order you to do things. Some of them might instruct you to "love your neighbour", whilst others will tell you to "burn his house down". Some people will try to rationalise this with the categorisation of "good" and "evil" spirits, but The Great Simulator only creates the illusion of "good" and "evil" for the purposes of making the experience more compelling and interesting. Therefore, please avoid being judgmental.

Your human consciousness will experience wanting to do "things". Examples would be, marrying someone, buying something, joining a religion, etc. It is important to have these feelings or desires; otherwise you will tend to do nothing. There are a host of spirit forms that help you have these feelings and, hence, encourage you to act. Many people can even consciously sense spirit beings actively encouraging them to do "things".

These spirit beings can only succeed because you want to do that "thing" in the first place. They work by encouraging your self-justification process, in effect, they take a small desire to experience something and turn it into a large one.

Obsession

This is where God has got a "bad name". Mention God in the western world and "half" the people around you will instantly think you are suffering from wild delusions. To be fair, extremists of various sorts have used the "God ordered me to….." or "doing God's work/will" self justification on so many occasions that adverse publicity was bound to result.

People who stand on street corners, armed with a megaphone and or some pamphlets, telling you to love Jesus, Mohammed, a prophet or even God, enjoy their work. They do so because it makes them feel better. They feel an uplifting energy flowing through their bodies. Combined with the sense of purpose that accompanies this activity, you could prescribe this as a treatment for depression.

The misconception that arises is as follows; just who or what is inspiring you to become a religious fanatic ? Many years ago I, was ambushed by an African woman who was giving out religious pamphlets. Out of curiosity, I stopped and talked with her for a few minutes. At this point, I spotted that she had an "earthbound (= stuck)" deceased monk's spirit inspiring her to do her work. I could see this spirit telling her what to say, though I don't think she had the slightest idea where her inspiration was coming form.

In some cases you will find spirit beings having a conversation with these sorts of people. As, in particular, Lower Spirit Beings are very adept at confusing and misleading unwary human beings. You really have to use your own judgment about who you are connecting with. There are plenty of "impostors" or "mimics" out there. In this case the lower spirit being was a remnant of a human monk, and therefore not a full human consciousness. Later in this book I will outline a few approaches to determining what you are communicating with.

In general, the majority of people who experience the urge to "serve God" do so in a quieter and more productive manner. However, as such good deeds tend not to generate scandal and intrigue, their good work goes largely unnoticed.

God's Will

Is to go around cruelly killing each other...... Well not quite. Ultimately the actions of human consciousnesses, which remember only exist in The Great Simulator, do not matter. It would be fairer to suggest that God has created The Great Simulator to "See what happens IF......"

To make it more interesting, the Earht plane was designed so that there would appear to be forces of "Good" and "Evil".

Now as both forces were created by God, it is unreasonable to suggest that anything "Evil" is there against God's Will. If you are confused about this, the only answer is to see it for yourself from the Astral World, then you will know exactly what I am writing about.

Saying anything is against God's Will, or God's Law, or even simply against God, is a massive misconception. One that God clearly wanted many people to have.

God (the real you), has allowed you to have a variety of experiences through human consciousnesses, the greater purpose of which we will look into later. Meanwhile, please be aware that your divine inspiration can drive you to commit what might be categorised by other human beings as "Evil" acts.

Good & Evil

"Good" and "Evil" are two sides of "the same coin". It is ultimately the same energy or force that can be applied in different directions. It might benefit you to have an alternative definition that will make more sense.

A Greater Awareness Force

You could call this the "Good Force":

- You can connect to a wonderful unconditional love.
- You can connect with your guiding spirits more easily.
- You enjoy a greater self-awareness.
- You become aware of the simulation you are experiencing.
- You recognise sustainable "win-win" solutions to your "problems".

A Reduced Awareness Force

You could call this the "Bad force":

- This makes it possible to dislike yourself and other people.
- Your consciousness becomes dominated by Lower Spirit Beings.
- You will tend to think more at the expense of being self-aware.
- You now tend to believe you are a human being and take yourself seriously.
- The "solutions" you see to your "problems" are unsustainable and create further "problems".

Now without this "Reduced Awareness Force" you could not have the Earht plane experience you are having. It enables you to be subsumed into the illusion that you are a human being. There would be no challenge to experiencing this life.

As you progress in your observations you will discover that these two forces are the same. It's your human consciousness's response that determines which one you will experience. In the end "good" and "bad" are merely a matter of perspective.

Your Divine Power

You experience this every day. Sometimes you feel an energy to "do something" which may be as mundane as going for a walk. If you go for that walk you will feel happier, healthier, and more aware. This energy is everywhere.

I recently walked into a bookshop and noticed a large hardbound book with a title similar to; "There Is No God". One of the great things about The Great Simulator is that especially on the Earht plane you can actually manage to ignore the continuous presence of God, the super-consciousness, in everything. It is a very amusing feature of the illusion, that human consciousnesses, experience.

If you really wanted to find a largely untapped source of this divine energy, just notice what is in the air you breathe.

The divine energy encourages you to "do things". As you become more self-aware you begin to appreciate that, for example, murdering other people or committing other acts of cruelty are not that "smart". The Great Simulator allows you to do just about anything you choose. Greater self-awareness discourages you from harming your fellow creations.

Final note: The categorisation of Groups 1, 2, & 3 is a simplification to assist your awareness and not a doctrine.

Exercise

Feel the divine energy that courses through you. Depending on how you react to it you will feel uplifted or depressed, happy or sad. The curious thing about this force, is that your response to it can produce a spectrum of results. For example, the feeling to "do" or "not do" something turns out to be the same force interpreted differently.

Next time you have a feeling that you cannot do "something" you need to do, try to convert that same feeling of "cannot" into "can do". Later on I will give you a fuller explanation of how to do this. Meanwhile you should try this for yourself. My tip for you is that this transformation is very easy to do, when you keep it simple.

14 Purpose & Illusion

Basic Principle

You are really an entity that cannot normally "see" itself.

For example, could something "white" see itself if all it could detect is more "white" ? Lacking any form of contrast, self awareness is difficult.

Therefore, contrast is necessary.

From the perspective of "black" it is much easier to detect "white". This is why the real you created "black".

To see yourself from the perspective of "black", you have to become "black", which is how you have come to experience being something that you are not. In this case you will tend to think that you are a human being.

Meanwhile, you find yourself so occupied living the very compelling illusion of living in the "black", that you now tend to ignore the "white".

Now add a further layer of contrast. Suppose that "black" appears to be composed of solid matter, whilst "white" appeared to be composed of nothing at all.

In this situation, if you live in the illusion that you are composed of "black", then "white" would appear to be vacuous; i.e. nothing there.

By this means, sensing what you really are is initially very very difficult.

The challenge is to help your human consciousness / illusion recognise what it actually is.

You Can Sense What You Are

At the moment your human consciousness sees and senses many things that are illusory. Therefore, all you have to do is "strip away" everything you are not, then the real you will be all that is left.

Your human consciousness does not relate to the idea of being "nothing" very easily. This chapter is here just to get your human consciousness familiar with some basic principles. By following these principles and the accompanying exercises you will begin to reveal your true self.

Why Your Human Form Exists

Let's look at the basic principle in more detail.

In your natural Super Consciousness state you cannot really see what you are or sense yourself "properly". As you are composed of a "nothingness", recognising what you are presents a few practical difficulties.

Being a creative entity, you have a solution….. Create an amazing "mirror".

You have therefore created a mirror that is not you, but which you can use to see yourself.

Now the “mirror” will appear to have some “form” or “mass”. The mirror can, and will, also relate to anything that has “form” or “mass”.

To begin with, the mirror only tends to recognise itself but, after a while, it comes to recognise that something created it. It realises it did not create itself.

To see you, its creator, the “mirror” gradually discovers how to recognise what is “mirror” and what is “not mirror”.

Progressively, the “mirror” recognises everything that (the real) you have created. Amazingly, its ability to experience the illusion also includes an ability to see through the illusion. The “mirrors” ability to be fooled into believing the illusion is also its ability to see through the illusion. It can do both. Read this paragraph a few times.

When the “mirror” recognises everything that is an illusion, it can also recognise what is not an illusion and, therefore, what is left. By recognising everything that is not the real “you”, the mirror can see you. You could consider it to be a process of elimination.

To summarise:

1. You can’t recognise what you are.

2. But you want to recognise what you are.

3. So you create a “mirror” that is the opposite of what you are.

4. As the mirror develops sufficient consciousness it notices that it simply could not have just created itself one day by "accident".

5. It then begins to recognise that something else created it.

6. By recognising how everything that is "not mirror" must be you, it begins to recognise what you are.

7. By this means it is possible to recognise "something" that can initially appear to be "nothing".

8. For you to see what you are, you look through, or experience, being the "mirror".

9. Even though the "mirror" does not really exist, by creating the illusion of a "mirror" you can "see" yourself. A mirror, after all, is an illusion mechanism that incidentally turns everything back to front.

10. The purpose of "The Great Simulator" is to make a "mirror" appear to exist so that you can recognise what you are.

11. The human form reading this book is just one small part of the "mirror".

12. Because your human consciousness experiences the contrast of having "form" or "mass", it can actually recognise something that has "no form" or "no mass". This is something you cannot do in your normal state as you have "no form" and "no mass".

13. What, you, the reader, are experiencing right now is a part of the super consciousness (God) looking at what you are, through this “mirror”.

14. As the experience can be confusing, you created various form of guidance to help yourself manage this feat, including, of course, this book.

Example

Let’s borrow a very simple example. Suppose you were pure electrical energy. Now you can’t see electricity, but you can see its effects:

- You can see lightning. However, you cannot see the actual electricity, only the light that it creates.

- We recognise electrical power from an electric motor, yet once again you are unable to see the electricity.

Scientists have learnt, little by little, to “see” electricity by studying all of its various effects. By studying everything it does, they have learnt to substantially recognise what it is.

Therefore, if you were electricity and you wanted to know what you were, it would make sense to create and experience being a scientist. By this means you would then have a better idea as to what you were.

Divine Energy And Inspiration

In the last chapter, I said that you could feel divine energy everywhere. However, now that you have read this chapter, you will be aware that the divine energy you can feel is actually a "consequence" of but not, actually, the Super-Consciousness, or God.

Divine energy is everywhere; nothing in The Great Simulator can appear without it, yet, you can only actually feel the consequences of its presence. As part of your understanding of The Great Simulator and the illusion you are experiencing, you need to recognise this.

Side Effects Of This Experiment

A "human" fixation on recognising "form" or "mass" is essential, as the end result you desire can only really be achieved through a process of elimination. That is why human beings are very interested in things with physical form and mass such as cars, money, and manifestations in general.

A human being who never recognised anything would never fulfil its purpose. You first have to study what you are not, before it is possible to recognise what you are. So you need some interest in what you are not, which is, of course, your human form.

Remember, to see what you really are, requires a sort of process of elimination.

To make this experiment work it is vital to have the necessary desire. So human consciousness generally needs to want to be solid and own solid things. Human consciousnesses, therefore, want to be born into human bodies and own solid possessions. If none of them had that desire to begin with then their purpose could not be fulfilled.

Everyone, in the human sense, who is alive, wanted to be alive, although few human beings in the "developed world" recognise this fact.

Desire for wealth and physical possessions

This is a simple side-effect that most human beings in urban environments experience. Even most of the "spiritually" or "religious" minded ones experience a strong attraction to physical wealth and possessions.

Ultimately, the degree to which a human being does, or does not, accumulate wealth and physical possessions is immaterial; all that the human being has to do is recognise what it is, or rather what created it.

Failing to see God

With the design of human beings making them fixated on "form" or "mass", it is really no surprise that some of them do not recognise that they are really just one (physical) formless entity experiencing a powerful illusion.

As you learn to recognise what you are, you will comprehend the formless being you really are. Indeed, human beings who believe that there is no God are merely commenting on what they correctly perceive.

Human beings who believe God, or the super-consciousness, does not exist, have got it completely back to front; they are the ones that don't exist.

Suffering

Human suffering is one aspect or "side effect" of this great experiment in awareness.

We will look at this more later. In the meantime, try being open to the likelihood that human beings are designed to cause themselves suffering, so that they will be more curious and inspired to investigate what they really are.

Do not get confused. Human beings are not created to suffer. They actually choose to suffer because it is one of the principal mechanisms they use to make themselves pay attention. Paying attention to what they are, is what they were created to do.

You cannot ultimately force a human being to do anything. So forcing them to recognise what they are through, for example, "compulsory religious teachings", only serves to demonstrate the pointlessness of even trying to do so.

Encouraging them is far more effective. Suffering is a great form of encouragement.

You And Your Illusion

People often say that if they had all the information and direction they needed, then this would solve most of their problems. You, unless you are skipping pages, now have a good insight into your purpose. But has it made a difference ?

The truth is that knowing what to do next, and having the energy to do it, are two entirely separate things. For you to follow your purpose, you need the energy to do it.

The following exercises, in this book, will connect you to more of the energy and awareness you need. Later on, you will become more aware that this is achieved by encouraging you to block yourself less.

You cannot ultimately solve the problems and challenges you face until you recognise why you wanted them in the first place.

Perhaps it is your destiny to run off and spend the rest of your human life worshipping yourself, as you are, after all, an aspect of God or the Super-Consciousness.

Alternatively, you might have a family to support, and/or valuable gifts to share with the society you live in. In that case "running off" would not help them and, ultimately, yourself. There is, after all, only one of us, and everyone you help is a part of you.

The likelihood, for the typical reader of this book, is that right now you face various challenges. Similarly, there may be goals you are trying to achieve.

The purpose of the exercises in this book is to help you recognise the illusions that limit your progress. Similarly, in recognising these many illusions, you will gradually recognise what you really are and achieve more of the things you want.

Exercise

See how many people you can assist in spotting everyday illusions.

Try doing this in a practical way that gives the people you help an immediate direct benefit that improves the quality of their lives. Doing so will alert you to the many ways in which you can immediately improve the quality of your life.

DO NOT try to force other people to read this book. Well, you can if you like, because this is not an instruction, it is a SUGGESTION. So if you do think someone else should read this book, try limiting yourself to suggesting it.

Neither should you (another suggestion) make this book a secret. The more people around you who are aware of the amazing illusions you are all experiencing, the easier it will be for you to notice the illusions that block your progress. This is why you should share your insights with those who are interested.

Again, balance this with the fact that everyone wants to be in an illusion to some degree. If you deny people all their illusions, you can block their inspiration to recognise what they are.

Doing this exercise will help other people. In helping others you will accelerate your own progress dramatically. Do (suggestion) give it a try.

Practice seeing common illusions

A great illusion you can help people recognise is the difference between what they think they want and how they actually behave.

People are always trying to achieve things:

- Making more money
- Getting jobs
- Finding partners
- Losing weight
- Etc

Spot the frequent examples of what people say they are trying to achieve versus the reality of what they are actually doing.

For example, people often say / think that they want to be happier. However, observations will demonstrate that these same people are very busy making themselves unhappy.

15 Apathy & Humour

Truth

The Truth is hidden by Apathy (can't be bothered to look) and can easily be discovered with Humour.

People often want to know answers:

- Answers on how to solve their "problems".
- Answers to why they exist.
- Answers about how to be smarter and more successful, etc.

Here is the funny part.

I have learnt how to connect to clients with their "Higher Selves", about which we will talk more, later. Anyway, their Higher Selves often give me more incisive and practical solutions and answers to their "problems", that they could ever hope for. Guess how the client often responds........ By yawn and starting to fall asleep.

It could be that I am a very dull and boring person. Yet strangely, whenever that person asks the same question, they yawn and start to fall asleep again, when the (generally very short) enlightening answer comes. It is a repeatable process.

If that person was alone and asked himself/herself that same question, he/she would have a hard time knowing the answer because he/she would instantly become either tired or distracted. His/her self-awareness would all but vanish and he/she would never know the answer.......... It would be swallowed up by a yawn.

You can solve this problem using humour, and in this chapter we are going to look at how to do precisely that.

Who Do You Think You Are Fooling ?

One of the biggest jokes you will persistently see, from the Astral level, is that virtually everyone you will ever meet, including yourself, is frequently doing precisely the opposite of what they say they want. In Part 1 of this book, I said that people think and talk a great deal of nonsense, to themselves. To be more accurate I recall that the word I used was "rubbish". Its time for you to recognise that you have been believing your own "rubbish".

The Great Simulator's Earht plane was designed so that you would be able to act in incredibly stupid ways, and never notice what was really happening. This stupidity is only possible, when you take yourself seriously. When you take yourself seriously you are unable to see the most incredible "jokes" and hence the truth of the matter.

Most of us will often say that we are trying to achieve things but, if you looked at our physical actions, you would see behaviour that has precisely the opposite effect. Doing the last exercise would make you aware of examples such as:

- Saying that you wanted to be richer, whilst avoiding actions that would make you richer.
- Saying that you wanted to be happier, whilst depressing yourself through unhelpful self-criticism and belittling.
- Saying that you wanted to have a better relationship with someone, yet continuously annoying that person.

- Saying that you wanted to fitter, yet actually avoiding most forms of exercise.

- How many examples can you add to this list right now ?

Similarly, people want to know the "Answers" to questions, yet they pay no attention to why, by skilfully lowering their awareness, they are actively choosing not to know the "Answers".

The truth is that you are creating your own reality and hence life. Everything that happens to you happens because you wanted it to. You have made it possible to NOT notice this by engineering an apathy towards the Truth.

Who are you fooling…….. Mostly yourself.

You Actually Want To Have "Problems"

Grasping this causes many people endless difficulty. Your brain will tell you that you do not want many, or all, of the "problems" or challenges you face. What your brain is telling you is an illusion.

This subject has been mentioned before, and it will be explored in greater depth again. The reason for mentioning it, so often, is that the illusion you are experiencing is so powerful, it takes you a while to see the truth for yourself. If you do not get endless reminders, you are actually pre-programmed to forget, so please understand why they are vital to your development.

"Problems" or challenges, inspire you to pay attention to what you actually are.

Recognising that you wanted to experience "problems" or challenges is the most effective way to solving them. You have to shift this desire from your sub-consciousness to your consciousness. Then the "problem" or challenge stops being your enemy and becomes your inspiration.

Wake Up

The morning of writing this section I opened a newspaper to see a wonderful story about a man who had allegedly eaten himself to an incredible 250kg (40st/550pounds). According to the newspaper report, he was blaming the local council (local government) for his condition. They had apparently made him a prisoner in his mother's home by refusing to pay to have the front door of the house widened. This man claimed that as he could not "get out" and exercise, this was causing him to become a human "fat mountain".

Picture this enormous fat man who could barely move, stuffing his face with food, whilst blaming the council (local government) for his plight.

This story raises two issues:

1. We ignore our own actions whilst blaming others for our plight. Consequently we continue to make the same "mistakes" until we take responsibility for our own actions.

2. We also get others to assist us in our "stupidity". In this case the man's mother must have been feeding him colossal amounts of food. If she had just stopped, presumably at some point he would have got thin enough to walk through his front door and get to the local food shops himself. In which case the local council would now not be required to widen the front door.

Be honest. Spend a few minutes, right now, noticing a few occasions when you have abdicated responsibility for your own actions. Similarly, notice how you support other people's illusions.

Why Being Serious Blocks You

When you are being "Serious", some amazing things happen within your thought process:

Your awareness reduces

You start to eliminate "apparently" irrelevant information from your mental calculations. So you now only see a very small and incomplete picture of reality.

That is not to say that information eliminated by your brain is completely irrelevant, rather, it is actually inconvenient.

Your subconscious desire to have "X" problem takes over

Let's say that you subconsciously want to feel stressed. Then in a state of reduced awareness you will start to find thoughts that make you stressed.

Possibly, the desire to solve "X" problem could be accompanied by a desire to experience being ruthless. In that case your thoughts would again busy themselves analysing why you should be ruthless in order to solve "X".

Self justification

When you want to experience "X" problem, your thought process will support you with enthusiasm. You will have probably noticed that such thoughts are "circular" in that they keep on coming back to the same position. This process enables you to self-justify your position and feel that "you are right", because you will keep repeating the thought that "you are right".

Locked Identity

All of a sudden you are locked into the position where you keep on experiencing the same limited personality. Your thought process keeps on telling you that you are someone trying to, in this case, solve "X" situation.

Blocked

Now obviously, if you are locked in the identity of being a person trying to solve "X" situation; you are not being the person who has solved "X". You are, instead busy being the person who CANNOT solve "X".

When you take yourself seriously, you lock yourself into a personality that will frequently be busy creating "problems", whilst unwilling to accept, and ignoring, the solutions.

Humour

You cannot change your thinking without changing the emotional desires that drive it.

Your thinking provides you with an illusion. Yet, if you noticed the desires you were also experiencing, you would see that your real motivation is often to accomplish the opposite. You do not notice these desires because you become absorbed by your thought process and rationalisation fantasies.

Whenever you view your human form from the vantage point of the Astral World, there are many things that are very funny to observe. You will laugh, when you see all the things you complain or get upset about ARE actually being created by you. You will cry tears of amusement, when you recognise the consistent effort you have put into blocking yourself.

This may seem surreal and unlikely, until you have experienced it for yourself. Having helped many clients do this, their first reaction to observing the truth is surprise, followed by laughter.

When you are being too serious your brain is pre-programmed to create powerful illusions. That is, after all, what you wanted.

If you want to be incredibly more insightful and capable, be prepared to recognise the humour in any situation.

Staying Awake

Connecting to the solution to your problems when you are occupied creating them puts you to sleep. Your thought process will wander and the most irrelevant of distractions will catch your attention. By "sleep", I mean that you might look awake, but your awareness will be at such a low level you might as well be having a comfortable sleep in your bed.

That is why, when my clients ask profound questions whilst not really wanting to know the answer, at that moment, they yawn and daydream. However, when they become aware of what had just happened, they laugh, wake up a little more and we try again.

It's not enough just to know the answer to something. You might believe that your life would be improved if you knew the answer to "X, Y, and Z". If we spent a few minutes chatting together, I could shock you with the number of great solutions to problems or challenges you claim you want to solve, and yet you actually know the answers to them.

The real challenge is not to find solutions; it's to stop ignoring them. You ignore solutions by putting yourself to sleep (even though you might outwardly appear to still be awake).

You can tell if you are asleep in relation to any challenge by one simple test:

Are you trying to "fix" or "do" something that appears unreasonably difficult to accomplish ?

If you are, then the probability is that you are asleep in relation to this challenge. To wake up, just start to notice how you actually wanted to be in that position. You WILL need to use your sense of humour to do this.

Apathy

If you wanted to hide the "Secret of the Universe", you would have to do no more that cloak it in apathy. Anyone who got near it would instantly lose interest in looking for it and wander off in another direction without ever finding it.

The illusion of human life you are experiencing is made possible because you (the super-consciousness) have energised your human consciousness with forces that make it apathetic towards noticing the greater reality.

Some people will even find their minds wandering when they read this page.

I often find that people are far more interested in being upset than recognising the solutions to their "problems" and challenges. When you recognise this happening to yourself…….. laugh.

The apathy you experience can come in subtle and cunning forms. By paying attention you can often see it in action. For example, when you are trying to solve a "problem" or challenge, notice how your rationalisation process is governed by your feelings. You will recognise solutions, yet feel you do not want to adopt many of them.

One of the amazing things about a human being is its ability to proclaim that it is rational, whilst actively making virtually every decision on an emotional basis. You employ apathy to actively avoid taking actions which would solve your "problems" or challenges. If you use some self-awareness you will spot this happening on a daily basis.

To see through this, we are soon going to look at one simple approach that is largely immune to apathy……. Better breathing (see next chapter).

In the meantime, to support better breathing, let's complete this chapter with a humorous exercise.

Exercise
Create Fewer Problems For Yourself

You give yourself problems so that you are inspired to wake-up, notice what you are, and connect to your higher abilities. Once you are more awake, you do not need that problem until you fall asleep again.

There are two simple parts to this exercise.

1. Humour

Next time you are trying to solve a "problem", notice everything you are doing to create it.

Not what others are doing.

You are doing.

Learn to laugh at the ridiculous situations you create or reciprocate (recreate in response to someone else's initial stupidity).

2. Apathy

Apathy towards solving "problems" is easy to spot in others. You are not that different. Learn to spot yourself being apathetic towards actions that would really help you. Use the ridiculousness of other as inspiration.

Observe how you can be apathetic towards acting differently.

Observe how you can be inspired towards taking actions which are bound to create problems for you.

The most materially successful people on the Earht plane are amazing problem solvers.

The more problems you solve, the more successful you become in an Earhtly sense.

Problems help you develop.

16 Breathing Is The Key

This is incredibly simple and totally underrated. At the end of the last chapter I pointed out that the answers to the things you wanted were hidden with apathy. We are now going to investigate how the simple act of breathing "properly" can make an incredible difference to your whole life. Try to avoid letting apathy take this gift from you.

When you have learnt to breathe better you will know two simple facts.

1. The principal illusions of The Great Simulator become possibly less blinding if you breathe "properly".

2. You wanted to have "blocked" breathing in order to experience the illusion of living as a human being.

Health & Strength

Breathing allows you to perform an amazing biological feat. It is the basis for all human physical life. Here is a quick explanation of how it works.

Your body contains carbon based physical energy. This physical energy is stored as proteins and fats in your body. You get this physical energy from eating plants, or animals that have themselves eaten plants.

Plants are principally constructed from carbon. They get this carbon from the air. Whenever you next pass a mighty tree, remember that almost the entire mass of the tree has been literally sucked out of the air. The tree sucks carbon dioxide, that's carbon plus oxygen, out of the air. Then the tree turns the carbon into wood and leaves. The oxygen is ejected as a waste product. The tree is basically a big lump of carbon that was entirely extracted from the air. Vegetables are the same, principally carbon, but with a higher water content.

When you breathe, the purpose is to convert the physical energy stores in your body into movement and airborne carbon. You achieve this by inhaling oxygen, passing it through your blood stream and collecting up the carbon. You then exhale the carbon plus its carrier, the oxygen, as carbon dioxide.

The system is incredibly efficient and is used by all animals. You eat carbon, then convert it into physical energy by breathing it out.

The more you breathe:
The more physical energy you can access.

Bonus feature:
You can slim and loose weight simply by breathing better as fat is exhaled as carbon.

If you want to do more of nearly anything, then it involves breathing more.

Therefore, if you can learn to breathe better, you are instantly able to do more things.

One final point. Having more oxygen in your body assists your body's immune system and healing ability. One reason is that oxygen is actually poisonous to many of the things that can damage your body. Evolution has designed the human body to have a high tolerance to oxygen poisoning, whereas bacteria, for example, generally have a low tolerance to oxygen. Breathing better is very good for you.

How To Breathe Better

I am going to make this very simple. That should overcome many of the limitations of telling you how to do this exercise through a book. One to one lessons are better, but a book is what you have today. So lets get going….

Now unless you have already been trained in breathing the chances are that you are using the "wrong" muscles to do it. This may come as a surprise to you, after all, you have managed to survive this long using the "wrong" muscles. But you will probably have been doing a "Blocked Breathing".

Blocked Breathing

Now I know that there is really no right or wrong, but the expression is currently useful. Look in a mirror whilst wearing no clothes on the top part of your body. Alternatively, just wear something tight fitting.

Look in the mirror and observe how you physically breathe. If you breathe by moving your chest up and down then you are doing Blocked Breathing.

This occurs when the muscles you should be using have become incapacitated as a result of you experiencing too many upsetting emotions. If you are, principally, breathing in a way that makes your chest move up and down, then this is the back-up system that keeps you alive. Appreciate this back-up system, you need it.

The muscles you should be using

Are located between your lungs and your intestines. They are known as the diaphragm muscles. Singers and athletes generally know where they are.

To find them (again) you simply pull your stomach IN and UP. Then push them DOWN. Perhaps you can even push your stomach out a little. Play with these muscles until you can easily get them to move. Occasionally clients have had trouble finding them, but in the end everyone succeeded.

As you practice you will find that you have a large breathing muscle at the bottom of your rib cage. It is typically about 30cm or 1foot across and is located at the bottom of your ribs. But as most people in the developed world do not use this muscle, it can appear to be solid and immobile to begin with.

Getting the air in and out

You can do this lying down. But you will learn faster if you do it sitting up straight on the front edge of a chair:

1. Keep your chest raised at all times.
2. Start by exhaling. Using your diaphragm muscles push the air up and out of your body.
3. Now inhale. Relax the diaphragm muscles and very, very, gently pull the air back in.
4. Repeat this.
5. Do not drop your chest at any time.

Improving the technique

For the typical person you should now be letting in approximately 3 times the original volume of air into your body. In order not to hyperventilate (which makes you dizzy), you can now breathe 3 times slower.

1. Gently breathe in seeing how far down into your body you can pull the air.
2. Pause.
3. Gently exhale most of the air.
4. Pause.
5. Repeat.

Practice this until you can do it without having to think about it.

Hands and feet

When you have got your breathing working so that it needs minimal attention, you will have the spare capacity to add some useful features.

Become aware of your hands and feet connecting with the Earht. As getting you "out of your head" and into the rest of your body is the goal, being aware of your hands and feet makes this much easier.

Smiling

If you are doing this breathing exercise "properly" you will feel yourself smiling with no effort. As you are learning how to breathe properly, you are probably not smiling and or feeling happy. Don't try to force yourself. That would be stupid.

Your smile is an indicator of success. So forcing yourself to smile is simply cheating yourself and wasting your own time. Here is how to get your smile:

Reposition your centre of awareness

Place your attention just below the level of your belly button. Imagine yourself looking out at this level until you can stay out of your head. Then keep your attention at this level without imagining anything.

Practice breathing with your attention just below the level of your belly button.

How do you feel

This part confuses many people at first. With the centre of your awareness now much lower in your body it is possible to feel the emotions your are experiencing more accurately.

You might find that you feel incredibly happy or sad. Though, typically most people do not feel much at all to begin with. That is because you have suppressed your emotions. Suppressed emotions feel like a "flat line" or not much.

As your emotions are determining most of your thinking, there are obvious advantages to knowing what is going on inside.

Get some life in

Again, this may take practice. When I am working one to one with a client, what you are reading in this chapter takes approximately an hour to "get right". Lacking one to one expert help, it will probably take you even longer. If you think you can do all this in five minutes, you are either an expert or an idiot, I hope expert.

The "flat line" feeling can be relieved by reducing your muscle tensions in your lower abdomen (that's approximately just between your hips). As you reduce the muscle tension, your breathing will start to feel more pleasant and you will start to smile.

Success

To explain success, it can help to recognise “failure”. Someone once said to me that they had practiced for an “hour”. This person had a stressed and unhappy look, which told me everything I needed to know. However, the person in question did not appear to have grasped that something might have gone “slightly” (or completely) wrong.

Keep on going

When you are doing this properly, you won’t really want to stop. You will be happy to do it all day. Breathing this way will make you smile and feel happy to be alive.

Typical Mistakes

Here are a few signs that you need to practice more:

- Saying: “I can’t do this all day”. This person is suggesting that it is better to go through their day with unhappy breathing that will cause them to under-perform in a variety of ways. You should be able to gradually automate better breathing without it being an effort.

- Saying: “I have too many things to think about”. Firstly: The point of practicing is to automate better breathing, so there should be no need to think about it all the time. Secondly: Arriving at excellent solutions, to most challenges, requires very little thinking and lots of inspiration. Better breathing helps you think less, connect to answers more, and should give you an easier day with less effort.

- Saying: “I have too many thoughts in my head”. Is a sign that you are truly overcome by the illusion of Earht life.

If you did the breathing exercise described in this chapter, your head would "go quiet". Presumably that is what was desired ?

- Trying to force your breathing while centred in your head. Try doing this deliberately to gain a quick understanding of why that causes problems.

Success

You feel happy to be alive and energised to do interesting things. You will smile effortlessly.

Persistent Failure

Now that you have some idea of what success and failure feel like, it is worth giving you a simple tip that will solve most failures.

Remember the last chapter on humour. Do you remember how we looked into the subject of how being too serious actually makes problem-solving more difficult ?

The problem

You try to breathe better, but it just does not feel that great. Then your mind starts wandering and the whole exercise becomes a big effort.

The solution

Acknowledge and celebrate your success. In The Great Simulator we tend to talk a lot of "rubbish" to ourselves. We think we want to be happy and successful, etc……When actually we often want to be the complete opposite.

When you practice better breathing, you run straight into your subconscious desire to be somehow "blocked". The mistake is to fight that feeling. Make that mistake and you WILL lose. If you don't believe me, go ahead and do battle with blocked muscles and emotions. Afterwards, you will know not to waste your time in future.

The answer is to find any "blockages" you discover amusing. Amusing in that you will have spent a great deal of time talking "rubbish" to yourself about not wanting "blockages", whereas, in reality, you had been spending a great deal of time creating without noticing. The trick is to laugh at your own "stupidity".

Once you learn how to laugh at how stupid you can be, you will find these blockages just melt away. Now that is being very clever.

WHY ?

One great reason for having "blockages" is to teach you not to take yourself seriously. Your sense of humour will set you free, and you will have great breathing.

Exercises

Keep practicing breathing properly until you can do it effortlessly.

Practice doing it when you are "under pressure" and watch how easily your performance can effortlessly improve. In this situation you don't need to stay focused in your stomach / pelvis all the time, you will after all be needing your head / brain. The point of checking your breathing, and temporarily focusing lower in your body, is to clear "cluttering and confusing" thoughts from your head, so that you can be smarter and, where necessary, decisive.

If you are doing physical exercise or manual labour, etc, try breathing better and enjoy the results.

Learn to breathe better while speaking. It gives you a clearer more commanding voice.

If the exercises feels difficult you are making a basic mistake so re-read this chapter.

17 No Creative Visualisation

This chapter may or may not apply to you. Let's find out.

If you are one of those people who has a great deal of success practicing your Creative Visualisation, then carry on succeeding. Perhaps you could even skip this chapter, although, it does make interesting reading.

If, however, like most people, you have had limited success with Creative Visualisation, then pay attention.

Here is a simple analogy. People who are successful at Creative Visualisation are like skilled typists working a computer keyboard. Their hands are doing exactly what they desire and, consequently, their computer screens are filled with precisely what was intended. Meanwhile, the unskilled operator looks like someone, who instead of using their hands, prefers to use his/her backside (bottom). They bounce up and down on the keyboard randomly pressing the keys. As they are even facing in the wrong direction, they do not even notice the pathetic results they are achieving.

Simple test

Do the majority of goals you visualise become reality ?
(This includes fantasies about the future)

If not, then carry on reading.

The "Problem"

Visualising anything in your "head" can often be counter productive. Your brain works like a calculator. It works out if your plans are viable, or if they need improvement. However, it can also ignore important factors.

For example, if you are going on holiday, your brain is very good at working out what items you should pack. It will plan and calculate what you are going to need. It will even make contingency plans about what you might need, which is why we often travel with unnecessarily overweight baggage. Nevertheless, a brain normally does a very good job for the average holidaymaker, so no great problem here.

Next example. If you are trying to anticipate correctly everything you need on your holiday, while avoiding taking anything you will not need, this is more complex. To do this accurately, you basically have to be "clairvoyant" and see your own future. You have to see what will happen, as opposed to what you think will happen. Your brain may not anticipate that you should bring the inflatable beds which will be needed when your airline has problems, and you have to spend the night sleeping on the floor at the airport.

The challenge is that your brain frequently DOES NOT sense the "invisible force" that creates future events. Some times it does, but often it will not.

From time to time, you will sense, correctly, that something is "going to happen", even though you have no physical evidence. This is an example of when your brain correctly includes the "invisible force" in its calculation and, thereby, arrives at the right answer.

In contrast, when you are day-dreaming, you tend to be highly disconnected from the "invisible forces" that determine whether, or not, a goal is even possible. Hence, visualising your goal can blind you to the impending reality.

Why Day-Dreaming Is Counter Productive

People who are trying to achieve their goals by day-dreaming are, normally, actually delaying the achievement of that goal.

Day-dreaming is something you do when you are bored, or do not like yourself. You day-dream by disconnecting from your body and floating off somewhere "nicer". In practice, your consciousness could be found on the Low Astral.

Achieving a goal is going to require, presumably, some form of physical action. On the Earht plane, physical action is "king". In other words, in this part of The Great Simulator actually taking physical action has the biggest effect. This may appear obvious, but the number of people who think that they can achieve things, by doing little more than thinking about it, is incredible.

At this stage I would like to take you even further, in your understanding of how most things in The Great Simulator are actually "back to front". If you, the super-consciousness, did not want your human form to, for example, win the lottery, day-dreaming would be an excellent way of achieving that. You would simply inspire that human form to have a pleasant relaxing day-dream about how wonderful it would be to win the lottery. The day-dream, could be made so pleasant and relaxing that the human form would not even bother to go to the shops and buy a lottery ticket. However, that same human form would actually believe it was taking steps to win the lottery. What an illusion !

This book was written to help you navigate The Great Simulator. In so doing you will be able to enjoy the illusion of achieving more things on the Earht plane. For some people this could be enjoying the illusion of physically being a multi-millionaire on the Earht plane. Whatever, you desire, within reason, you can probably achieve it on the Earth plane, if you pay attention.

Day-dreaming is not paying attention.

Force For Change

If you, the Super-Consciousness, want your human form to achieve something, you simply inspire it with the divine energy to do it, and it will (probably) happen.

In this situation, the human form will suddenly start visualising that it wants to achieve something. Armed with the energy to do it, it will normally succeed. End of story.

You, the human being, should already have begun to notice that sometimes there can appear to be an "invisible force" for action that drives your successes. When that force is not present, not much happens. If you have not already noticed this, then this would be a good time to start.

Your human brain, that calculator which thinks that it is in charge, actually has no access to these "invisible forces". It experiences the consequences of them and works with them, but it does not control them.

Real Creative Visualisation

What you will generally experience

You, the human consciousness, will get the feeling you want to achieve something. You will see a picture of that thing. You will take physical steps towards achieving that thing. Done.

To begin with you may just sense the goal this "invisible force" is helping you achieve. Sometimes you may write the goal you sense onto a piece of paper. Whatever the case, you will normally keep the goal in the forefront of your consciousness.

The traditional principle of creative visualisation is that by creating "whatever" you picture in your mind, you can achieve it. The reality of the situation is that unless the force for action is there, you are just day-dreaming.

Real creative visualisation is where you feel, or sense, that force for action and as part of the process of achieving "whatever" objective, you picture it.

The illusion of creative visualisation is that you think that you can achieve something by picturing it in your mind. If the force for action is not present, visualising it makes very little difference. For that "invisible force" is your divine Free Will.

Furthermore, your Free Will does not always turn out in the form that you, the human consciousness, might anticipate. On some occasions attempting to achieve the goal may turn out to be a "disaster". An example would be Captain Scott's failed attempt to reach the South Pole and get back alive, but that would probably have been the "Grand Design" and ultimately a perfect end to the story. Therefore, take note that the outcomes of what you visualise are not always what you originally imagined.

What you are capable of

This book was written to help you, the Super-Consciousness, experience FREE WILL whilst in your own Great Simulator. This book is a message to yourself.

In order for you to control the forces for action, that make creative visualisation successful, you need to have access to your Free Will. It's your Free Will that is really deciding whether or not your human form succeeds, or fails, at anything. The sooner your human consciousness recognises this determining fact, the sooner it will achieve its Earhtly purpose.

To access your Free Will on Earht, you have to recognise what you are.

An important step, towards recognising what you really are, is recognising your divine Free Will in action. It is a force that brings you both important win-win successes and temptation.

Many people have recognised that they can access their Free Will on Earht and achieve, for example, wealth, the lover of their choice, etc. There is no good or bad in this respect. However, you should be wary of starting to believe that your human form is real and therefore, somehow separate from the super-consciousness. Such a confusion makes you "cling" to your human identity. If you do that, a "fall" becomes inevitable.

As a safe and pragmatic way forward, simply notice how your Free Will is actually guiding you, and work with it.

In the next chapter we will look into a few more techniques which will help this human consciousness wake-up and access it's Free Will more easily. Meanwhile, here is a simple exercise to practice, that helps you work with the existing Free Will.

Exercise

As previously pointed out, successful creative visualisation is actually riding an invisible wave of Free Will. This wave provides the energy for something to happen.

If the energy is there for an event to physically happen, then your visualisation will become a reality.

If the energy is not there, your visualisation will remain a fantasy.

- Practice noticing when that energy is, or is not, present.

Simple.

18 Switching Off The Noise

We previously looked into the subject of the Special Effects Team, the lower spirit beings who make you think you are a living human. To enable you recognise their presence you were given directions on better breathing, and cautioned about the Creative Visualisation illusions. These components are required for this next evolution in your awareness.

In this chapter, you are going to learn how to see important aspects of the illusion you are experiencing function in real time. Once you have succeeded, it is hard to go back. The illusion, that you are your thoughts will be permanently fractured. After this chapter, your sense of identity will have to be re-evaluated.

The Illusion Of Thoughts

One of the simple reasons why you will, initially, have extreme difficulty accessing your natural Free Will is that you think you are your thoughts and emotions.

Normally, you will have a whole series of thoughts streaming through your head. If you try to meditate, it can be very difficult to quieten them, as they "have a life of their own".

Just take a moment to notice how there is a constant "chatter" or "conversation" going on in your head.

An expression I once heard which captured the peculiarity of the human mind was the "Monkey Mind". Considering the randomness, or repetitiveness, of this "noise" in your head, it is amazing that you are ever able to focus effectively on anything.

In Chapter 5 on the Special Effects Team you were made intellectually aware that a team of lower spirit beings were determining what you feel and think. In practice, most people initially react negatively to that proposition. However, rejection or denial is precisely what these spirit beings want.

Do you remember that anything can be hidden in Apathy. Your human consciousness is pre-programmed to seek Identity, and to resist the proposition that it does not really exist. Consequently, you won't want to believe that the thoughts and emotions you consider to be "You" are an ingenious and varying invention.

This tendency gives the lower spirit beings, what would be considered in baseball terms, "a home run". As the lower spirits beings purpose is to create an illusion, they normally try not to be recognised or detected. They can achieve this very easily as they control your feelings, which in turn determine what your rational brain believes. In effect, they ensure that you will not want to believe the truth. Thus, the illusion of your independent human existence is complete.

However, you the super-consciousness, would also like your human consciousness to wake up. At this moment you are allowing it an opportunity to see through the illusion.

Prepare

Do not try imagining any of what comes next. Your imagination WILL be inaccurate and, ultimately, misleading.

1. I am going to tell you what to look for.

2. If you do not see / sense it, do not try imagining it. Just try again.

3. The exercise is to allow impressions to arrive in your brain.

4. This exercise works much better if you are breathing properly.

Better breathing is the most important aspect to this exercise. If you really want to succeed, but have not regularly practiced better breathing, then practice your breathing before reading this section further until you have. The logic of why you should wait is as follows:

- You need a quiet mind to succeed. Better breathing is vital.

- You need to be in a wakened energy state. Better breathing is vital.

- You don't want your mind wandering off into imagination. Better breathing is vital.

We need to borrow the part of your brain that is otherwise amusing itself with day-dreaming and imagination. We need it to do what it was ultimately designed to also do.......... receive impressions consciously.

Your brain can receive impressions of things that are not physically on the Earht plane. This is a natural function of your brain that is neglected in many people. Your brain can actually "see" the Astral World. That is possible whenever it stops the internal noise and lets the impressions of the Astral World arrive.

Hello Team

Precisely how the Special Effects Team appear to you will be an individual experience, based on your conditioning. They are actually formless, but as you do not relate very well to that, they will appear to have some form.

As their job is to deceive you, be careful.

As their job is to make the amazing illusion you wanted to experience actually function, welcome them.

Sense…… Do not imagine

Allow yourself to adopt a warm unconditionally loving attitude. You need to breathe properly to do this. This cannot be forced.

Now, surrounding you are a number of what might be described as "elemental spirits". Most of them have been there your entire Earht life. Be loving, and allow yourself to sense their presence.

Form

How they appear varies from person to person. Here are some examples:

- Little monkeys
- Fish
- Pixies
- Birds
- Garden Gnomes
- Living Socks / Glove Puppets

Normally they should appear to be smaller than you. Technically, it is fair to say that at this dimension or level of the Astral World, they are much smaller than a human consciousness. This is because they form some of the basic components of a human consciousness, therefore they should be smaller. If they do appear larger, remember that their field of expertise is of course illusions.

Precisely how they appear will vary and is not important at this time.

Say “Hello” to the Special Effects Team

What you are doing

By sending them a warm, unconditional love, your head will start to go quiet.

But if you start to think or imagine anything, they will spring back into action.

To see or sense them, you need to have a quiet head.

More love

They are controlled by unconditional love. They are rendered invisible to your senses by denial. Don’t imagine them, just lovingly notice them. You do this by letting a warm, caring, feeling radiate all around you.

Their nature could be described as “playful”, but as long as you are being aware of them, in a loving way, they tend to go quiet.

Back to the illusion

To restart the "noise" or conversation in your head, that the Special Effects Team provide, you will find that any of the following normally works:

- Trying to push them away or get rid of them.
- Arguing with them.
- Imagining them.
- Blaming them for anything.
- Denying their existence.
- Or just letting them take over.

Now What ?

After a few attempts you will start to get the impression that something is there. Chatting with them is an odd experience, that will take you round in circles, as they of course are responsible for the creation of the entire conversation (there is no "you" talking). In practice you cannot really chat to them, as you do not have the power of conversation without them. This is because they create, what you previously would have considered to be, your personal thoughts.

Additional confusion arises if you ask them for the answers to your "problems" or challenges. Firstly, because you, as has just been explained, cannot really chat with them. Secondly, as their job is ultimately to mislead you and create a powerful illusion, what do you think will happen ?

To answer the question "Now What ?", the suggestion is that you should practice becoming aware of them. The logic of doing so is very simple:

- The fact that you are reading this book means that you want to become more aware of what you really are. Therefore, it is helpful if you recognise the illusion that makes you think you are a human being.

- Your human ability to deal effectively with your life's challenges is determined by your ability to adopt the appropriate identity. To switch on new abilities, it helps if, sometimes, you let go of some of your old personality or identity. Recognising that you only borrow manufactured personalities is helpful.

- Similarly, acknowledging the illusion helps you similarly recognise what you actually are which, of course, is now helping achieve the purpose of The Great Simulator.

Practical Application

Suggesting to a human consciousness that there are advantages to fulfilling its ultimate purpose, often results in the response that it has some more important practical problems to deal with NOW. The "my problems first and God later" attitude is, of course, part of the design of The Great Simulator. The Great Simulator was intended to enable you to ignore what you really are, and hence, how you came to create your human consciousness along with its associated challenges. Acknowledging that you have these practical earthly challenges to address, the exercises for noticing the lower spirit beings are intended to help you to actually resolve your immediate "problems". Therefore, developing yourself, and fulfilling the purpose of your existence, by paying attention to what you actually are, should be recognised as being mutually supportive activities.

Remembering what you are will help you solve any problem you choose.

Similarly it will help you accomplish anything else you choose (within reason).

Pick a problem to be solved or something you want to accomplish (that you think you need help with).
Then:

1. Notice your breathing.

2. Notice how your breathing is blocked.

3. Allow yourself to breathe properly.

4. Be loving to the Special Effects Team

5. Congratulate them for making your conscious believe that it was less capable than it really is.

At this point your Guides will be in a position to change your awareness. If you remember from Part 1, your guiding spirits are entities whose purpose is to raise your awareness and help you resolve "problems", etc.

You will then see "ways forward" because:

1. You let go of an old identity.

2. You experience the energy of a more "capable personality".

3. You briefly remembered what you are (even doing so to a small degree helps).

4. You now think in a more dynamic and capable way.

Solutions to two "difficulties" that may arise:

- If you are not succeeding with this exercise: As it has been made very simple, it is not that difficult to go back and check for "mistakes". If you pay attention you will find you made a mistake. Practice this exercise repeatedly and you will discover your mistakes.

- You will only succeed in this exercise when you successfully "wake-up". Hence it is only logical that should you go "back to sleep", then you will become less capable. It's easy for you to notice if you have gone "back to sleep", because the dynamic energy and awareness you will have experienced has now become a memory. Do not try to imagine the divine energy, just do the exercise again.

Exercise

Your human consciousness has been designed to have practical need of being more self-aware. Every time you use this greater self-awareness, it will physically help you in the simulation of your human existence.

1. Discover how much you can help yourself by unconditionally loving the Special Effects Team. Doing so makes it a great deal easier for your Guides to help you.

2. Practice noticing how the Special Effects Team do their amazing work. Keep practicing until you recognise that you are not actually your thoughts and emotions.

If you do this apparently simple exercise, you will be seeing or sensing a Lower Astral part of The Great Simulator in Action. This book did offer to enable you to do this. You now have very specific guidance to help you achieve this.

19 Embracing The Astral

To expand your "in the moment" awareness of how The Great Simulator is working you need to see or sense what is really happening. The exercise in the last chapter is designed to quieten your human mind sufficiently to allow you to see beyond the Low Astral. To understand how to apply that new awareness to Astral Projection, let us examine the human equipment you currently are working with.

The Equipment

Your brain

Is something you can do without ? Yes.

When you physically die, you do not take it with you; it gets buried or cremated, etc, yet you will experience being very much alive. This is one of the confusing things about death, you will experience being very much alive, yet the brain you are using, right now, will have ceased to function.

So what is it doing, right now ?

It is actually a sort of advanced calculator. You could say that it is a sort of adding machine. An advanced adding machine but, in truth, not much more than that. It does little more than process information. When you die, calculations such as mathematics become difficult, but your higher awareness actually improves.

When you project your consciousness onto the Astral, you can start to experience awareness without "a brain", but lacking your rationalising skills, you can get scared very easily. See "Project Heavy" at the end of this chapter.

Your imagination

You have the ability to imagine lots of things, for example, you could imagine a fantasy "other world". To start to see the Astral World you need to use the same parts of your brain that are responsible for imagination, but differently. There is a world of difference between seeing as opposed to fantasizing about The Astral world.

Your imagination is a powerful tool that is essential for your everyday Earht life. As we discussed earlier, you see everything in your imagination. Your physical eyes send electro chemical signals to your brain and, in your imagination, you recreate an image of the world you perceive around you. Your imagination enables you to navigate by sensing things.

You, well actually the Special Effects Team, recreate the impression of what you think you are seeing. This impression exists on the low Astral and is there for everyone on the Low Astral to see. There is nothing private about it.

Having better control over your imagination is vital for the "Project Light" technique at the end of this chapter.

Your consciousness

This is the bit that was formed before you were physically born, and returns to heaven when you physically die. It is a reflection of your real intentions or divine Free Will. However, a human consciousness does not actually have any Free Will, just the illusion of having it.

It is principally directed by your Soul, and constructed from Guiding Spirits or Guides. You could say that a group of Guides gather together and a human consciousness is formed. To make it even more interesting, the mix of Guides change throughout your lifetime. This is one of the reasons why, you, the human consciousness, do not really exist as a stable independent entity. Yes, there is something there right now, and it will be dismantled later.

Guides, in turn, gather together and act through the Special Effects Team or Lower Spirits. When a human consciousness is manifesting the illusion of living on Earht, it needs the Special Effects Team to gather and supplement its human personality. When that human consciousness returns to a higher Astral level (heaven), it dispenses with most if not all, of the Special Effects Team.

Let me give you a quick example that should help you understand. You could give a child some plastic playing blocks. A popular toy in this respect would be “Lego”. The child could make a house from the Lego. Then it could dismantle the house and build a car. The existence of the house and car would be transient or temporary. Similarly you, the human consciousness, will only appear to exist, on a temporary basis.

At the risk of getting “sidetracked”, don’t go thinking that you are nothing. You are a Super-Consciousness, or God, experiencing being a transient or really non-existent consciousness. Also note that there is only one God; i.e. Only one of us.

You are simply using a human consciousness to experience yourself from a radically different perspective.

The Relationship

The soul

Is an extension of the Super-Consciousness which directs Guides.

The human consciousness

Is built from Guides and higher spirit beings.

The imagination

Is built from The Special Effects Team or lower spirit beings.

The brain

Is built from water, carbon, and some other Earhtly stuff.

The Earht

Appears to exist by ingeniously "slowing down" energy. By doing so you get the very convincing illusion of physical matter.

The Relationship

You the super-consciousness, want to have certain experiences. That is your divine will.

The Guiding Spirits you created are a manifestation of your divine will. To get the experience to work they form human consciousnesses in the middle levels of the Astral World.

To get a consciousness to appear to be lower in the Astral World, they enlist the help of the Special Effects Team. At this point your consciousness now has a sense of independent identity, as it appears to have its own independent imagination.

The consciousness has not really gone lower in the Astral World, it in fact exists everywhere in the Astral World. It just appears to be lower in the Astral World. That is because it seems focused by the imaginative activities of the Special Effects Team.

To achieve the illusion of a human life, some of the more elemental members of the Special Effects Team have created the impression of cellular life forms. They are the ones who have created the individual cells that form a human body.

These "Cell Spirits" come and go on an amazing scale. Your human body is constructed from both living cells and their corpses. Most of your bone, tooth, nail and the outer skin cells are dead. Hence a significant part of your human form is constructed from corpses. Meanwhile, other parts are very much alive and your body would be in "real trouble" if too many of those cells died prematurely. Overall, it would be fair to say that your infant human body and your adult human body hardly have an original cell in common. So the very Cell Spirits that compose a human form come and go all the time.

The Cell Spirits are organised and marshalled into place, by The Special Effects Team. The Special Effects Team is directed by the Guides. The Guides are organised by the Souls (more on Souls in Part 3). And everything is inspired by your Free Will. That is the Free Will of you, God.

What Is The Astral World ?

The Astral World is basically everything except you, the super-consciousness. You created all these spirit forms and everything else in the Astral World. You are experiencing being everything in the Astral World, thus, everything in the Astral World is connected and your creation…… But not actually you.

This means that whilst you are experiencing being the person reading this book, you are also experiencing being each one of the cells in the body of that human being. In an ironic way, the cells in the body of you, the person reading this book, are under the impression that the human consciousness which created that body is God.

Anyway, the Astral World is a "mirror" that you the super-consciousness created to "look back" at yourself. At the top or Soul end, of the Astral World, everything is very connected and there is not much contrast, but in realms or regions such as the Earht plane, everything looks completely separated. Here, there is a massive contrast between what you really are, and what you are experiencing being.

The challenge you, the super-consciousness, are experiencing right now is that the contrast between what you really are and what you are experiencing is so extreme that it becomes disorientating. To reduce this level of disorientation, it can be helpful to occasionally remind yourself of the greater truth. Therefore, remember the Astral World and the consciousness in it were created by you, for your own benefit.

As your principal intention was to experience yourself from the viewpoint of, in this particular case, a human being, you will not want to spend all your time experiencing the Astral World. Conversely, you will want to spend your time experiencing the human world or Earht. To that end you have tied the human consciousness to its physical body with a "piece of elastic" or astral cord. This makes it difficult for the typical human consciousness to navigate the Astral World, as you wanted it to be largely Earht bound.

However, a completely Earht bound human consciousness will have no other experiences from which to recognise that it is not actually a human being. So anyone reading this book is permitted some degree of Astral Projection. Your only limitation will be the degree to which you, the human consciousness, can explore the "other worlds" whilst still taking an interest and active participation in life on the Earht plane.

Imagination Or Reality

Navigating the Astral World is initially not that different from navigation on Earth. To begin with, as on Earht, you will be using your imagination. So the next step in your human training is to comprehend the difference between "imagination" and "reality" (or, specifically, the apparent reality of The Great Simulator). This is a very important skill to have, considering you need to learn to navigate using your imagination. So let's understand the difference.

What is imagination

This is mostly the lower spirit beings having some fun. They are encouraged to do that and, it has to be said that, human beings who display little imagination are generally very boring people.

The lower spirit beings often will compete for control of the human consciousness by injecting various ideas, sensations and pictures into the human brain. The human brain duly processes as much as it can and then you will experience rambling thoughts. When your Guides take more control the rambling thoughts reduce and you will appear able to concentrate.

Imagination can be seeing or pretending to experience, anything. It is achieved by the Special Effects team creating a small mini-world in the bottom of the Astral World. These worlds are normally fleeting, though for "serial" fantasists, they can acquire considerable substance. People escape to these worlds they have created whenever they get bored with their Earht lives.

Fictional books are a good example of Earthly stimulation that assist bored human consciousnesses escape into imagination. The writer creates a fictional Astral mini-world and readers create their own replicas. Both writers and readers tend to do this because they get bored with Earht plane "reality". Someday I will probably do the same thing and we can all have fun in our Astral mini-worlds.

Reality

Let's call reality what we can agree on. Reality in this context is an interesting subject. As nothing in The Great Simulator is actually real, true reality is that there is nothing there at all. Meanwhile, all human consciousnesses will experience an apparent reality of what appears to be there on the Astral.

If the two of us (human beings) stood in the same room we could agree on what furniture was in the room. We would both be using our imagination which interprets our visual senses to see the room and agree how many chairs were placed in it. We similarly could agree on the number, sizes and shapes of any tables. That would be our reality, what we could agree upon.

Now when it comes to navigating the Astral World, I have taught clients to navigate it by sharing our experience of it. Using the same imagination we would normally use to see the physical world around us, we would explore the Astral World. Though, obviously not using our physical eyes in this case. By then comparing what we saw and sensed, we are able to agree on what we found. This enables us to explore the substantial parts of the Astral World, as well as more transient elements, or mini-worlds, created by fleeting imagination.

How you see on the Astral

This is so simple yet, initially, can be difficult to comprehend.

You stop creating your own mini-world.

Here is an analogy. Think of your imagination as luminous powder which glows in the dark. Suppose you were standing in a darkened room, you would not be able to see its contents. But, if you sprinkled this powder around the darkened room, it would cover both the floor and the furniture. By just letting the powder settle wherever it fell, you would see where the floor and furniture was. You would not actually be seeing the furniture, but your luminous powder would be showing you where it was.

Being imaginative, on the other hand, is like standing in the same room making your own shapes and patterns with the luminous powder. You could create lots of interesting effects, but they would have little relation to the reality of what was actually there. In this case you would be preoccupied with your own creations, and not notice the furniture.

If you spend your time playing with the "luminous powder", you only see what you are creating. In this case you would be creating your own mini-world. Conversely, if you stop playing with it, it immediately settles and suddenly you can see The Astral World. It is that simple, just stop creating.

However, under normal circumstances, the Special Effects Team will be so busy following your instruction to "create", that you won't appear able to just stop creating.

So could you see the Astral World right now?

You can, but you are also fixated by the physical Earht plane. As you are "closer" to the Earht plane you tend to give it "priority" and recognise it first. The Astral world is all around you at this moment, and you are, in fact, ignoring it.

Practical example. If you were reading this book on an aircraft flying at 30,000 feet, you would sense yourself to be flying by travelling on that aircraft. If you then sensed the Astral World you are actually in, you would find it to be more like being in a dark place (Low Astral), where you are surrounded by your Guides. You would then recognise that despite your Earhtly impressions of travelling, you were in fact stationary and going precisely nowhere.

Influence of the Guides

To see where you actually are therefore is a two stage process:

1. You need to stop imagining where you might be, and start noticing where you are.

2. You need to recognise that you are simultaneously experiencing being on the Earht plane and living in the Astral World. This ability is normally acquired by first

noticing the Astral World and then "overlapping" it with your physical impressions.

To achieve this, you obviously do not want to be wandering around in a rambling imaginative world of your own. You need the Special Effects Team to be "quiet".

Your Guides are there to inspire a degree of order. They encourage The Special Effects team to play at doing what the Guides direct them to. It's a bit like when a parent controls the game being played by children, order prevails.

The guiding spirits apply their unconditional love and the Special Effects Team "quietens". The human consciousness will now start to register what is going on around it, as opposed to the human consciousness focusing on the interesting fantasies and thoughts the Special Effects Team were providing. That is why, for example, very spiritual people can often appear to be very serene and composed.

Exercise

There are basically two approaches to practicing Astral Projection:

1. Project "Heavy". Which is very difficult to begin with for the typical reader.

2. Project "Light". Which is much easier. But you will have little idea what you are doing, so you might lose interest quickly.

This gives you an interesting choice between an approach fraught with difficulty, or one hindered by apathy, which is why most people never manage conscious Astral projection.

I suggest you practice both and in time you will manage to combine the two techniques. You can practice both exercises in parallel, but obviously not simultaneously.

You will also have vastly more chance of success if you have learnt to quieten the special effects team (see last chapter).

Project Heavy

Your physical body is modelled on an Auric or Spirit Body. This spirit body looks like an exact replica of your human form, because your human form is actually a replica of your spirit body.

Your spirit body already leaves your physical body, partially, every time you go to sleep. It leaves fully and permanently when you die. I can tell you, from personal experience, that if too much of your spirit body starts to leave when you should otherwise be alive, you get so cold that you have to stop. Your spirit body will only permanently detach when it is appropriate for you to die.

WARNING. If you have any sort of adverse medical heart condition this Heavy approach is probably not a good idea. You are likely to encounter some shocking surprises which frighten you and put your heart under pressure. You could die. However if you are healthy you should survive and you can send me an email about your experiences.

Here is the procedure:

1. Lie down somewhere comfortable where you are unlikely to be disturbed. Try to eliminate unexpected noises such as the phone ringing. Lying on your back is usually best.

2. Breathe properly.

3. Quieten the special effects team (see last chapter).

4. The difficult bit. You have to let your body fall asleep whilst keeping your mind awake. This takes a lot of practice. Good results are often obtained in the middle of the afternoon when your physical body is not expecting to go into a deep nocturnal sleep. A heavy meal beforehand increases the chance of going completely to sleep (not helpful).

5. SUCCESS comes in the form of paralysing yourself.

6. Paralysis. It is not as severe as it sounds. When you sleep, you dream (whether or not you remember your dreams). When you dream you move. To prevent you from injuring yourself, your brain largely disconnects your consciousness from your muscles. Otherwise, you would sleep-walk or, perhaps, even run with your eyes still shut. You will know when you have paralysed yourself because you will not be able to move your arms, legs, or even consciously control your breathing.

7. Shock. Suddenly being paralysed, is initially, an unpleasant experience. You will get a shock when you find that you cannot talk or move your arms and legs. So if you have a weak heart you could die but, if you are fit,

you should be ok. It's a bit like a really scary moment in a film.

8. Recovery. Instead of struggling to move your arms and legs, or scream for help, just move one finger; because your brain thinks you are in a dream state it will let you twitch. Moving a finger, or toe, restarts your muscle control and everything returns to normal. Then, after a few minutes, your heart will stop racing from the shock.

9. Practice sending your body to sleep until doing so does not "scare the hell out of you".

10. When you have got your body to sleep but kept your consciousness alert, you can float out of your body. You are out and off. The less effort you use, the better the results. This is something you have to get used to; on the Astral you are, in reality, weightless, hence effort, is actually counterproductive.

11. No need to go too far to begin with. Generally, try to stay at least 2 metres, or 6 feet, away from your body, otherwise you tend to get pulled back prematurely.

12. Returning to your body normally happens by itself. However, in the very unlikely event that during one of your initial Astral Projection experiments, you do not return to your body within a few minutes, you should do so consciously. You achieve that by simply lying down in you physical body.

13. Move a finger or toe and wake your body up.

14. Write down your experience.

15. With a little more practice, start to notice some of the other spirit beings that will be around.

The bit about being scared or frightened is difficult to convey, intellectually, in words. For various reasons, you are likely to get scared during your early projection attempts. The most common reasons are:

- You get disturbed by your lack of physical bodily control.
- You encounter something unexpected.

The things that are likely to frighten you are, of themselves, unlikely to actually harm you. However, a fearful reaction is the real hazard. Not having your intellect at your disposal, you can easily get frightened by events or encounters of an otherwise non-hazardous nature.

If, during your early attempts you do not get some really good scares, you are probably not projecting.

Fortunately, with practice, you get used to the very strange things you WILL encounter, and you won't be scared anymore.

Project Light

Sometimes this is known as remote viewing. This is easier to start with, but the results are initially less exciting and, hence, you may lose interest before you acquire any significant skill. However, this is, ultimately, an essential skill that will enormously benefit your development. So learn how to do it !

When you project Heavy, you take the greater part of your human spirit form. You will discover what it is to leave your body without actually dying, but with projecting Light, you only take what you need.

However, as you do not project very much of your human spirit form, you will wonder if you have projected anything. At this point a very annoying fact emerges; if you doubt your ability to project, that will suck what little of your spirit form you managed to project right back to your body. Very annoying.

Anyway, here is the procedure.

1. Sit somewhere comfortable. Distractions are not helpful for obvious reasons, but this is something you could practice while, say, waiting for a phone call.

2. Quieten the Special Effects Team (see last chapter).

3. Do not slump. It blocks your breathing. Breathing properly gives you the energy to do this. So sitting straight, relaxed and unsupported is normally best for this approach.

4. Be prepared for a different visual experience. Normally, you can physically see for great distances. On the Astral, to begin with it may only be a few meters or yards and it may be blurry or out of focus.

5. Close your eyes. Pretend you are approx 3 meters or 10 feet away and look back at your physical body.

6. Don't imagine your human body.

7. Just sense what you can. If it all appears indistinct, out of focus, or otherwise strange to begin with, that is an indication you are succeeding.

8. Keep practicing this, until the Astral image of yourself becomes easier to see.

9. Write down your experiences.

10. With a little more practice start to notice some of the other spirit beings that will be around.

As you progress with both techniques, they eventually start to merge. Welcome to the Low Astral world.

20 Navigating The Astral

Doing the last exercise requires persistence and bravery which, of course, make the fruits of your success all the greater. Now you can access the Astral World consciously, let's look at navigating it.

Navigation

Help from your Guides

Your Guides not only help you experience the correct state of consciousness to see the Astral World, but they also help you navigate it. As you, the human consciousness, have little idea where you are going, without help you are almost guaranteed to get lost.

This tends to happen because you will try to perceive the Astral World in terms of what you experience on the Earht. You will tend to behave like a child trying to force "round pegs into square holes." You will simply not recognise the Astral World the way it actually is, hence, there is a great likelihood of getting lost.

The technical explanation why you will tend to do this is very simple; you wanted to experience an Earht plane. A human consciousness is really on the Astral all the time, but its desire for Earht life is so strong that it habitually tries to convert everything into an "Earht reality". Remember, the "Earht reality" is, of course, an illusion.

Your Guides do not stop you wanting to experience Earth, they just quieten the Special Effects Team that provide the experience. Speaking from personal experience, it's not unknown for your Guides to occasionally pull you out of your human body, and into the Astral World. You will get quite a surprise if they do that to you.

Where am I ?

With the Special Effects Team quietened, you can notice that you are on the Low Astral. As this is an inherently dark place, you don't initially tend to see (actually, recognise) very much. At which point most people give up.

Now there are many ways to navigate on the Astral, and this description is only one possibility regarding what can happen. So remember, this is a guide and there are alternatives.

Assuming, you start to notice the "nothingness" around you, the next thing that tends to happen is that one (sometimes more) of your Guides will try to greet you. The experience can be similar to being in a darkened room and noticing there is someone else there, who you cannot quite see properly.

At this point the immediate differences between Earht and Astral experiences start emerging. On Earht it is possible to see a person in a room because of external light source(s) that illuminates them, whereas, on the Astral, it is your Guide that tends to illuminate the "room". Also, there might only be limited material for your Guide to manifest with, so you might only see half a body.

These meetings initially tend not to last for very long, as you will find that you either lose interest or get too excited, and start imagining things again. Before you know it you are back on Earht….. Again !

Moving Around

With a little practice the darkness of your initial Astral projections will appear to fade. This is a result of your recognising things you previously dismissed as irrelevant. Remember, your desire to experience being alive on Earht makes it, initially, difficult to see the reality of the Astral World.

Next, it is possible for you to recognise that you can move around Astrally. To begin with, it is generally best to practice moving around the Low Astral Earth Plane. This is the plane that is closest to the physical world so whilst different, it will, at least have some familiar reference points.

This Low Astral Earth Plane is very similar to the physical Earht and is the intention, or template, from which the physical Earth is modelled. It appears similar to Earht, but different. So you can visit Earhtly places, or people, and generally have fun.

Note that you will, sometimes, be visible to small children and domestic pets that are on the Earht plane. You can, however, influence almost anyone, even if they don't notice you, so consciously Astrally projecting yourself can have many applications.

You can basically go Astrally anywhere on Eahrt you want. Though the curious thing you will discover is that you will tend to lack some of your human abilities. It can, for example, be difficult to read. This is because, in a parallel to death, you can lose access to your calculator brain whilst projecting.

You will also notice that you are not bound by gravity, which is now "optional". Similarly, you will notice that you can travel at tremendous speed. There is also a good chance that you will be naked, but as intention becomes reality at this level, you only need to wish for clothes and they will manifest themselves.

I once found that I was Astrally manifesting a work bag I would carry when commuting. I had to laugh, because this black "rucksack-like" bag had, inadvertently become part of my human identity and hence appeared to be part of my Astral or spirit body.

If you want to know what happens to you when you die and get confused, visit a grave yard or mortuary. There you will tend to find an abundance of confused spirits. They have strange and interesting beliefs. Meeting them will teach you a great deal about how illusions can persist beyond physical death.

Whatever you do, it is difficult to actually harm yourself. Though as a passing story, in my "early days" of Astral projection I tried launching myself Astrally from an upper window of the house I lived in. As my desire to be on Earht was, subconsciously, still very strong, I inadvertently introduced some Gravity (you can get it near Earht). The result was that my Astral body plunged head first into the concrete floor of the yard below. I remember "bouncing". When I later returned to my body, I arose up with a headache.

You don't tend to see too much of your Guides, on the low Astral near the Earht plane. You would, if you looked out for them, but you tend to get absorbed by other things and hence not notice them.

There is one category of location on Earht that is, however, hard to visit Astrally; Alien cities. Much as people look for Aliens to come from the space, you should try looking on Earht as well. For some reason I have yet to research, they can often be found in the deep oceans. These cities do not exist on the physical Earht plane, so you will not find them with a submarine, yet you might find them on the low Astral near the Earht plane. However, most people who read this will never find such places, the alien residents are “fussy” about who they let in. Most human consciousnesses will never penetrate the strong defences they cunningly use which includes, amongst other things, apathy.

Moving Up

Once you have fulfilled your curiosity about exploring the Earht from the perspective of the low Astral, and assuming you overcome your curiosity about visiting “Earht Aliens” who would rather be left alone (don’t “push” this one). Then you can get on with spending more time with your guiding spirits.

Humans like the Earht reality so much that your Guides have used it to model some places for you to visit. Going to visit your deceased relatives is usually a good start, and this helps give you some experience of the different human heavens that exist. Depending on the various Earhtly culture and beliefs, the Guides have modelled a variety of heavens to match.

One common “mistake” is to make such journeys with the intention of getting one of your deceased relatives to sort the “problems” you perceive yourself to have on Earht. Doing so tends to reduce the degree of help you get and thus you tend to end up “back in your head” again. Whereas, if your intention was to become more aware about how you are creating a “problem”, you are far more likely to be successful. So instead of going on a “grumbling mission”, find out how your relatives are doing.

Having worked as a medium, I recall that once a female client asked me to find her deceased father. Finding him turned out to be relatively easy as he was in a heaven that was relatively close to Earht. However, he was unwilling to communicate with her, despite her demands for Earhtly advice, but this sort of encounter is the exception rather than the norm.

Generally speaking, any relative you will initially want to visit has probably been helping you on the Low Astral anyway, so you don't have to do much looking to find them. Get them or her to take you to one of the heavens and give you a little tour; meet some other relatives and Guides in the process.

The guides have also constructed mini-worlds that look like colleges, temples and other places of interest. So you can go there to educate and uplift yourself. The fabled city of Shangri-La is an example of a place you can, at last find. But being an Astral city, there is, of course, more than one version of it.

As you go higher in the Astral, the features, such as they are, tend to disappear. At this point, even though you won't be able to recognise much, you will still find plenty of people to visit. This is why it can take a little practice to visit a deceased relative who has abandoned his or her human appearance. However, it probably won't be too long before you get bored, by the featurelessness of these regions of the Astral World, and back to Earht you will go.

Noticing Guides

Between giving yourself minor Astral "bumps" which you will probably subsequently feel "back" on Earht, and generally getting lost, you need some guidance. Sometimes a Guide will appear to be a deceased relative, at other times a new and helpful friend.

Your guides are there to help you. As soon as you leave your physical body, you are in an easier position to notice them.

On the Astral, the "energy" of everything is much more apparent. In this case, Guides tend to radiate a warm unconditional love.

With a little experience and using some "common sense" judgments it is soon possible to determine who, or what is trying to help you, and conversely who, or what, is trying to deceive you. There are entities out there that may try to deceive the unwary traveller. But their "low energy" gives them away.

In that the low Astral is largely populated with entities whose job it is to deceive you into believing that the Earht is real, there are plenty of things out there that want to confuse you. In some instances it can appear that you are getting attacked. Though as fear is the principal weapon used against you, real harm is not possible (unless for example you have a weak heart and your human form dies of shock).

Your guides, however, are not of the low Astral and hence tend to radiate bright loving energies. Hence your Guides tend to look relatively bright in the relative darkness of the Low Astral. Experience will soon reveal who is trying to help you and who is "playing games". Don't worry about getting a little mixed up to begin with, it's all part of the learning and training process.

There is to some extent a law of attraction that helps you connect with your Guides, or miss them entirely. If your intention is to help others, your Guides will support you. If you have an intention to harm others, your Guides will try to discourage you by making you more aware. But if you find spirit beings willing to help you harm others….. watch out. For they are probably not your Guides and ultimately you will be the victim.

Working with your Guides

This is a pleasure you can initially first develop on the Astral. Get to know them there. Let them take you places and show you things.

Then the next part of the process begins.

Spending all your days Astrally projecting was probably not part of your plan for an Earht experience. So use your experience of Astral projection to recognise the presence of your Guides with you right now. They have been with you since before you were born, acknowledge them as the friends they truly are.

Exercise 1

What to do when projecting

Here is a list of things to try. You may or may not succeed as, for reasons previously outlined, you did want to experience life on Earht. The Astral World is such a huge and fascinating place that it can rapidly render the illusion of human existence an irrelevance. So most people won't get too far because it may interfere with your Earhtly purpose.

Anyway, see how much of the following list you can experience on the Astral:

- Get out of your physical body consciously.
- Meet some of your guiding spirits.
- See the Special Effects Team in action.
- Visit your deceased relatives.

- Visit people who will be coming to Earht (eg. Future children and grandchildren)
- Find some learning Astral places or colleges / temples.
- Visit famous Earht locations and see them from an Astral perspective.
- Travel beyond Earht.

In the process of doing this, try to also:

1. Get a real understanding that a human consciousness is only a visitor to Earht.
2. Therefore Earht is not actually your home.
3. Look up some previous incarnation links.
4. Investigate some future incarnation links.
5. Get your Guides to help you "see" the illusion of the Physical Earht Plane being created.
6. See how the illusion of physical birth and death is accomplished.
7. See how the illusion of physical challenges is created.

NOTE: Relatively few human beings will accomplish all these possibilities, and it could take a lifetime. So just do what you can.

Exercise 2

New link with your Guides

Practicing these exercises will have a profound effect on your everyday life. You will find that you can notice and communicate with your Guides simply by being aware that they are with you all the time. Once you have met them on the Astral, then practice being aware of your Guides and communicating whilst you are on the Earht plane. You will be aware that they are normally with you as you go about your daily business.

Caution

It is easier for one of the Special Effects Team to chat with you than it is for one of your Guides. Guides work predominantly through awareness, whilst the Special Effects Team use thoughts.

So first build a relationship with your Guides, on the Astral, where it is easier to know with whom you are communicating. Otherwise, you might be sending me an email along the lines of:

"*HELP. I tried to connect to one of my Guides, but now I have something talking in my head all day.*

What do I do next ?

Signed X"

The answer will of course be:

" Dear X. You are chatting with one of the Special Effects Team. Give it unconditional love and it will shut up".

Note that unconditional love, which often appears as a white, silver, or golden light, does not harm or silence your Guides.

21 Working With The Energies

A Great Misconception

As you will no doubt be aware, what you think you want and what you often actually receive in life can be two completely different things. Traditionally, most people are locked into a battle to get their life to conform to their desires. To that end they often work very hard on projects that ultimately fail.

No doubt you will have encountered such frustrating failure yourself ?

No doubt you will also have wished for Earht reality to conform better to your human desires ?

Such an attitude would, however, make it even harder to recognise the illusion for what it is, as we are about to look into why such thinking is completely "back to front".

Getting it the right way round

Now the simple logic we are experimenting with is as follows; instead of wishing that Earht events conform to your wishes, why not try the complete reverse of this.

The complete reverse being that the results you achieve to any Earht endeavour, or project, are always perfection, even if the result appears to be failure. So, instead of thinking that you are not achieving what you want, the reality would be that you are ALWAYS achieving what you want.

For example, if you spent years trying to get "your dream job", but failed, then that would be perfection. Even though, in this example, you will have experienced wanting to succeed.

It is your thinking that has become obsessed with the mistaken thought that you wanted a different outcome. Everything that happens on Earht is perfection and the consequence of your actual desires, as opposed to what you think you want.

To get your thinking "The right way round", you need to recognise that what you think you want and what you really want, are frequently complete opposites. This is actually easier than it may first appear, all you need do is start recognising that "outcomes" are the consequence of your real desires.

Recognising Earht The Way It Actually Is

It might appear that your Earht life is somewhat pointless, when you take the view that the result of whatever you attempt is always perfection. Pointless because, if you never exerted yourself at all that is also perfection..... So no point in doing anything ?

Fortunately, you are unlikely to escape the inevitable feelings of frustration you are bound to experience, if you adopt such a lazy attitude towards your human existence. If you did take this approach, the frustration you are going to experience will inspire you to pay some attention to what is actually happening.

Assuming you avoid delaying your progress with such an attitude, you can speed up your development by simply getting on with "life", using a more aware attitude. Let's summarise, and then try a new approach:

Old way of thinking.

I try to do something and fail.......... The world is not perfect and I have failed.

New way of thinking

I try to do something and fail......... Because that is what I wanted.

In this case it is because I wanted to experience failure.

New logic

- You want to have certain experiences such as success or failure.
- To achieve those experiences you have to make your body desire to embark upon them. Otherwise, in the case of the failure experiences, you would never embark upon them.
- This makes it possible to succeed, or fail, as you ultimately desire.
- What your human consciousness thinks it wants is not the determining factor in the apparent success of any project.
- All the experiences you have are designed to encourage you to be more aware.

Example

Your human consciousness might think it wants to have a fantastic loving relationship with someone, whereas, you actually want to experience having a terrible relationship ending in a messy divorce.

In this example, getting your human consciousness to desire a happy relationship is an excellent way of ultimately experiencing the "horrors" of what will result. Dealing with such "horrors" will give you new experiences, and awareness, you would not otherwise have had.

Example

Death: Most people do not want to die. Yet physical death is an important and ultimately enjoyable experience for most human consciousnesses. Because death can be so pleasant, it is better to give your human consciousness a fear of death. After all, you did want to experience Earht life.

If you were to remain locked in a human consciousness for too long, you really do start to become "Earht bound". Death is a natural means of returning you to a less artificial condition. But to stop you leaving the Earht plane too soon, a fear of death is very helpful.

How to see the greater reality

There are essentially two approaches that work:

Firstly.
You could just say that the truth of what you wanted can be determined only by your actions. What you think and say you want is irrelevant. However, this has the disadvantage that you only see the greater reality in hindsight.

Or
Secondly.
You could become aware of what you are creating in the first place. This is practically impossible to ever see from the low level of the Earht plane, but much easier to see from the Astral World.

Advantages Of Astral Projection Skills

The main advantages of mastering the last chapter on the Astral World are:

1. You begin to experience some very different "realities". Hence you can recognise what is actually happening much faster. Seeing the greater reality of your actual desires is only really possible from "outside your head". For whilst your brain is an amazing calculator, it is also responsible for making the illusion of Earht life incredibly real.

2. You cement a practical working relationship with your guiding spirits. This is vital, as otherwise you will tend to think "nonsense" to yourself and remain locked in illusions. The role of your Guides is, amongst other things, to help you in recognising the greater reality. Because, unlike your human consciousness, they are not locked into an illusion and, therefore, remain aware of the greater reality.

The difficulty most human consciousnesses have in seeing The Great Simulator in action, is that they are preoccupied with thoughts and fantasies that maintain the illusion.

Normally, you do not see that you are in an illusion because you find the illusion too interesting and or compelling. If you still don't believe that this is the case, then notice how at least one of the following list applies to you:

- Have you ever read an interesting story in a book, or magazine, and not wished to be disturbed ?

- Have you ever been irritated by someone disturbing you while you were watching a television programme ?

- Have you ever paid money to see a film or movie ?

- Have you ever paid money to buy a book, or magazine, that contains interesting stories ?

- Do you get annoyed if you are interrupted whilst having an interesting conversation with someone ?

Now all of this may appear to be very obvious and everyday. Yet it is ignoring the very obvious that makes the illusion you are experiencing function, so notice how you enjoy illusions and fantasies.

Living With The Illusion

Don't fight it

Fighting the illusion you are experiencing will in fact actually make it stronger. One of the main illusions most people experience, is the view that they did not want to experience that same illusion, in the first place.

Instead, be amused and congratulating.

Incidentally, I know that the next sentence is repetitive, but you need all the reminders you can get. Imagining you are experiencing an illusion makes the illusion stronger and reduces your Earhtly capability.

Link with your guiding spirits to keep you more self-aware

The last chapter gives one of many approaches to building an Earht relationship with your Guides. Keep on developing this. Remember that in most cases they make you aware, and, generally, in short bursts. Whereas, if you find that you have an easy "chatting all day" connection, you have probably (unless you are very experienced) connected to one of the Special Effects Team.

By paying attention to spending less time imagining things, you can easily be more aware that you are simultaneously on the Earht plane and the Astral. A simple way, of making this heightened awareness more stable, is to keep noticing that your guides are present with you all the time.

The typical "mistake" that makes such a heightened awareness "hard work" is not actually connecting with them. To perform this mistake, notice that your Guides are with you, but skilfully avoid connecting to their unconditional love and humour. Successfully making this mistake will soon have you immersed in the imaginative thoughts and emotions supplied by the Special Effects Team.

Divine "Trouble"

The paradox

Here is an example of how many people think:

So if there is a divine and loving God, why does he allow so much cruelty and suffering to occur on Earth. In particular, why do I have to suffer and endure so many problems and hardships ? If there really was a God then all this suffering and injustice would end.

The logic

If you connect with your Guides, they will confirm this:

Most people in the "developed / urbanized world" only attempt to link or connect with their guiding spirits, Angels, Jesus, Mohamed, Buda, Krishna, etc, and or God, because they are upset and have a problem. A problem they want help resolving. They rarely make the connection just to say hello and "Thanks" for the amazing experience.

People tend to drift around, sometimes being very busy, but actually in a walking sleep state. The purpose of human existence is ultimately difficult to fulfil whilst asleep. So as problems and challenges tend to inspire the human consciousness to wake up and make the heavenly connection...... Then it is logical to inspire human consciousnesses to choose to give themselves problems and challenges as part of the waking up process that fulfils their purpose.

The confusion

Unsurprisingly many people are of a view that you should worship "God or one of his prophets", etc. They believe that they will be "rescued" or "saved" from their difficulties if they do so. There is even occasional evidence that this approach can be fruitful.

The point of this book is that paying attention to what you really are, and what is going on, will help you. So the principle behind worshipping and getting "rescued" or "saved" is therefore easy to understand.

The confusion occurs when you start thinking that "God or one of his prophets", etc, is about to save you from some difficulty or other. It's not unreasonable to think this, but because this thinking and understanding contain "errors", the results of worshiping and praying are haphazard. The principal "error" is to see God, or the Super-Consciousness, as something separate from yourself.

Believing that you are separate from the super-consciousness reduces your ability. It makes you deny your innate natural capabilities. It causes you to wait until someone else sorts out your challenges, that is the road to more "suffering".

However, this is, after all, the illusion you wanted to experience, then overcome.

The Great Simulator was designed to create this confusion. You could say that "this is part of the FUN". Behaving as if you were a separate entity from God, is deliberately intended to cause you a great deal of confusion.

Question for you
Is it really necessary to pray to yourself, for salvation from situations you have created for your own ultimate benefit ?

Or
Are there better alternatives ?

Divine Power

Free will
This book is here to help you reconnect to your Free Will. To access your Free Will you need to step out of the illusion The Great Simulator creates on Earht. That is only possible when you recognise that you truly wanted to experience it in the first place.

This recognition is not an intellectual experience; i.e. thinking "Yes, I wanted to experience the Earht plane, etc."

As you progressively recognise the greater reality that you wanted to experience on the Earht plane, you will also experience an inner "knowing" accompanied by a highly energising force. It is very easy to tell the difference as "knowing" is a very "physical" experience.

If you have been practicing connecting with your Guides properly, you will know exactly what I mean.

Recognising your divine power

You have experienced desires to do things and take actions, such as go to the shops or telephone someone. It seems perfectly normal and will often appear dependent on your "mood" or the inspiration you experience. This is your divine power flowing through your human consciousness. Without it you would not even be able to breathe.

You will have probably also noticed that these feelings often appear to have a life of their own. Now you may think that you can control them. Yet the inspiration to want to change or control them in any way is, of course, also your divine energy.

Therefore, almost anything you do is the result of Divine Power. At this point it should be becoming obvious that you, the human consciousness, do not normally appear to have any Free Will.

Seeing this from the Astral

Your thoughts are the consequence of your Free Will, but as a human consciousness you mostly experience the consequence of your Free Will rather than any actual control of it.

The way forward is to become significantly more aware of the process that is occurring. To have any control, you at least need to be aware of what is happening right now. This is where having some Astral Projection skills becomes essential as the Earht plane is designed to function as an illusion.

Instead of just experiencing the consequence of your Free Will, would it not be interesting to "see" this divine force acting upon your human consciousness in real time ?

Working From The Astral

Is easier than it may first appear. The essential skill in Astral Projection is the ability to focus your consciousness anywhere else apart from your head. As most human beings in the developed world are expert day-dreamers, this is merely modifying an existing skill.

All you need to do right now is practice seeing your human form from another view point. This could be from the corner of a room your body is in. Just practice seeing your physical body from a short distance away.

How your Astral World experience helps

One of your brain's great abilities is to ignore information. Astral Projection helps you practice noticing things you are normally ignoring. Otherwise you would see nothing at all of the real Astral World.

Avoiding a simple mistake

If I asked you to see yourself from a short distance away you would be tempted to imagine doing so. You would recall and try to recreate some memories you have of, for example, seeing yourself in a mirror.

That would be the mistake.

Don't try to imagine what you think is there, just use your Astral Projection skills to actually do it.

What you will see

If you have been practicing your Astral Projection then you will see yourself from an Astral perspective and you can move on to the next section.

If you have not been practicing your Astral Projection, or only doing so to a very limited degree, then here are a few tips that will to some extent compensate. To begin with, many people will not see anything much at all, whilst those who do will initially tend to imagine and not see.

If you do not practice you will never perfect this. Practice seeing yourself from a short distance away, right now. If you avoid the common mistakes, you should start to experience something similar to the following:

1. In some cases everything may appear dark to begin with.

2. You will not tend to see yourself in sharp focus.

3. You will begin to notice other energy forms around you.

4. You will probably notice that your human body is surrounded by an illuminated aura.

5. With a little further practice you will be aware of some energies flowing in and out of your body.

The next mistake

It is a little unfair to describe what tends to happen next as a mistake. It would instead be more accurate to describe it as a feature of your desire to experience the Earht plane, to the exclusion of recognising the Astral World.

When looking at your human form from a distance you soon get bored and become apathetic towards continuing. Now most people could look out of a car window for an hour without significant distraction. Yet it would be difficult for a person who has spent one hour gazing from a car window to spend one interrupted minute seeing their human form from a short distance away.

This example actually demonstrates something you may not have previously noticed. If you are looking out of a car window your attention jumps between what you are physically seeing and other things you are imagining. It is, in fact, extremely difficult for you to stare out of a car window for any length of time, without simultaneously starting to visualise other things in your mind.

When you are practicing this "remote viewing" or Astral Projection to see your human form from a short distance away you will rapidly encounter boredom. That is because when you do this exercise the Special Effects Team starts to become redundant and hence bored. They love their work, and they will rapidly apply themselves to the task of giving you a few things to think about or imagine. This is why it was hard to see yourself for very long to begin with.

Using The Help

Your guiding spirits are there to assist you, as opposed to solving all your "problems". They work by helping you be more aware, to achieve this, they encourage the Special Effects Team to be quieter. This makes it possible to "see" instead of imagining.

The energies

If you ask a guiding spirit what you, the human consciousness, really looks like, they would make you aware that:

1. You are a moving cloud of multi-coloured energies.
2. Which is under the impression that it is a human form.
3. And generally self-obsessed (that being part of the design).

Whilst you, the human consciousness, perceive events happening to you on Earht, your Guides would see something different. For them it looks like you, the cloud of energies, is simply changing its colour and shape. Not much more.

So, in order to help you understand what is actually happening, your Guides are helping you relate to the Astral world, where the events you experience are being created.

To some extent your Guides can see the physical world that you, the human consciousness, are experiencing. They can normally see it from a Low Astral perspective which bears a resemblance to the Earht plane, you think you are experiencing. So keep recognising that what you and your Guides relate to can be fundamentally different.

Aura

You, the human being, perceive yourself a solid entity. Your Guides perceive you as a cloud of coloured moving energies.

A human being that has practiced its astral awareness can see its, or other people's, auras. It's as if the human body is radiating clouds of coloured energies.

Meanwhile, for the Guides it's the other way round. You are a cloud of energies, which produce the impression, or illusion, of a human physical existence.

Guidance

As you practice seeing yourself from the perspective of the low Astral World, you will notice how different many things are. For example, you will notice how energy forms merge with each other, whereas on Earht, everything appears very solid and does not merge with other things that easily.

Meanwhile, more fundamentally, on the Astral you won't recognise what you are "seeing". Now, this would not present too many difficulties, except for one of your brain's excellent abilities; to ignore information. As your brain is quick to discount and ignore anything it deems irrelevant, if you do not recognise what you are seeing, you tend to ignore it altogether, thus you stop "seeing" and sensing.

Your Guides are there to assist you. They help you become aware and recognise what you can see and sense. This helps you to see more, by ignoring less.

If you have practiced connecting with your Guides on the Astral, you will be aware that they do not actually talk to you.

Instead they make you aware of what they are saying, it's the Special Effects Team who put it into words. This may appear to be a strange distinction, but it is one you need to have a practical familiarity with.

If you pay attention to the presence of your Guides, they can help you understand what you are seeing. For example, you will have already encountered the concept that all human beings have auras; perhaps, you may even have read a book on the subject, etc. Whatever you may have heard from others, or read about in a book on the subject of auras, what you actually see on the Astral, will always be different to what you might imagine whilst reading a book.

Your Guides can help you understand the practicalities of what you are looking at and sensing. Because, as just described, what you expect to find and what you will actually find are different. Your guides will help you become aware of what to look for and hence they gradually give you an in-depth understanding of many new subjects.

Hence, even though you will see and sense energy forms in different ways to other people, your Guides help you understand and interpret whatever you are detecting. Furthermore, they will also try to make you aware of things you had never previously considered, which is where it can get really interesting. Your Guides will teach you, and help you develop new skills that are highly relevant to your Earht life.

Exercises

Get used to how your aura changes

Your aura is not a constant entity; it fluctuates on a constant basis. Practice seeing your human form from a distance and hence your aura from a distance.

Try to avoid attempting to alter your aura to begin with, just practice noticing it. By practicing this exercise at different times of the day, and in different situations, you will soon begin acquire a practical understanding of what colours and shapes relate to how you feel, and what you are capable of.

Look at other peoples auras

Practice this a lot. People can try and hide their feelings or intentions, but their auras are there for all to see.

Notice what the auras of trustworthy people are like, similarly observe the auras of less trustworthy individuals. Then, when you meet someone for the first time, you will have a practical database of previous observations upon which to be able to predict how someone will tend to behave.

Keep aware of your Guides

This is the key to really getting good at this subject. Your Guides will always be there trying to help you, that is why you will often find that you suddenly, “know something” you had no prior knowledge of.

Learn to recognise the difference between the useful, informative and highly accurate information that your guides give you, and the deliberate fantasies and illusions the Special Effects Team sometimes happily supply for your entertainment. If you practice this you will find that by enjoying and reliably connecting with your guides, you can pick up a great deal about any new subject, very quickly.

Avoid demanding reassurance

Your guides can help you become aware of whether, or not, a particular venture is likely to succeed. Practice sensing what is likely to happen from an Astral perspective.

Conversely, do not DEMAND to know "what will happen next". That actually lowers your awareness and hence hampers your development. Instead, just practice being aware.

Try not to interfere

It's actually quite easy to change your aura with a moment's thought. We will be looking into how to make changes. However, to begin with, you may see something you do not like in your aura. Naturally you will want to change it, and with a moment's thought the thing you don't like will be gone. Gone until you stop paying attention, when it will simply reoccur.

Actually, don't take my word for it. Try to change your aura as much as you like, but see if that really affects the quality of your life.

The point of the exercise of "not interfering" is to get you familiar with seeing and sensing what is going on, without attempting to change something you may not initially like. As you progress, you are going to find powerful new uses for the energies you might currently avoid. So, when you practice, just be aware to begin with, which is why this chapter was titled "Working with the Energies".

22 Recognising What You Wanted

Note to the reader:
This chapter focuses on the activities of the Special Effects Team who are responsible for your thoughts and feelings. They often like to remain unseen. It was difficult for me to write this chapter. Then, my principal editor found it physically hard to edit. It is very possible that you, the reader, may encounter unexpected difficulties. Should you find that, for whatever reason, this is a difficult chapter to read with a bright and clear mind……… you were warned !

Basics

For the typical person reading this book, the experience of life is approximately as follows:

- You appear to be alive on Earht.

- To some degree you will by now have become aware that you are not a human being, rather you are experiencing life as a human being.

- The human existence is very compelling, absorbing and demanding.

- You will probably have entertained the thought that it would be nice to have the time to really notice what you are. However, in many ways, you are a busy person and there are lots of Earthly concerns, issues, demands, challenges, etc, that have to be addressed / solved / etc….. First

Wrong

In order to get you, the human consciousness, to really start paying attention to what you actually are, you have been placed on what can best be described as a "hamster wheel". In other words, it does not matter how hard you do, or do not, apply yourself to the Earhtly demands……….. You are actually going nowhere.

Furthermore, you will probably not have truly recognised that all the challenges and experiences you are having only exist for the sole purpose of getting you to pay attention, to what you really are and what you actually want…… Not what you think you want.

Round & round

Many people live with a belief system that has the following key features:

1. Trying to get through this life as best they can.
2. Basically waiting to die.
3. No intention of returning to Earht again.

Meanwhile the reality is that once their human consciousness is lifted free of the illusions of human life, that same being will most probably want to return to the Earht plane again. Presumably, to have another life of not really going anywhere.

Greater reality

Whenever you think and believe that you are a human being, you will tend to be gripped by a compelling belief that you have to achieve things, whatever they might be. To be fair, if you truly attempted to do nothing, including feed yourself, you would, probably, soon suffer a physical death.

If you remember what you really are you will recognise that achieving things on Earht is having fun. But ultimately you are achieving nothing. It's like playing a computer game. The achievement only exists within the confines of the game.

Purpose

So human beings are going "round and round" on their "hamster wheels" of lifetimes, or incarnations, basically going nowhere in a simulator where they can ultimately achieve nothing and yet, this is wonderfully perfect.

The Earht plane allows you to have the most amazing experiences, without ultimately doing yourself any harm whatsoever.

Going back to the start of this chapter, it was pointed out that most people consider themselves too busy to pay attention to what they really are. Fortunately, the universe in which they live has been furnished with a great abundance of TIME.

Take as long as you want.

You have as many incarnations, or lifetimes, as you need, to notice what you really are.

In the meantime you can occupy yourself resolving more or less the same difficulties one lifetime after another.

Eventually you will……..

Wake Up.

Wake Up

This book repeatedly points out that your human consciousness is experiencing a powerful illusion. You will have been absorbed by this illusion for years and it, constantly, finds dynamic new and ingenious ways to convince you that Earht life is actually reality.

You will, of course, attempt to compensate for this by imagining and contemplating that you are in an illusion. However, such use of your imagination is an illusion in itself; this is another reminder to save yourself time and just pay attention.

As you are experiencing an ongoing powerful illusion that you are a human being and the Earht is real, this book has to constantly remind you to notice that it is not. At such moments it is helpful if you try and actually notice at least some aspect of the illusion. What do you notice right now ?

The next step in your progression towards waking up is to help your human consciousness to remember what you actually are through becoming more aware of what you really want. That will give you something to notice without the need for imagining.

Quick exercises summary

So far we have looked into a variety of techniques that enable you to break out of the illusion you are experiencing:

- You were shown how to breathe in a way that makes you significantly more aware.

- You have been given exercises that help you recognise how the thoughts and conversations in your head are NOT you and can be switched OFF.

- You were given directions on how to sense, see and hear your guiding spirits who are here to assist you.

- You have just been given (last chapter) an exercise that helps you see the energies you are experiencing which determine both your behaviour, and what happens to you in this physical life.

Are you becoming more aware ?

Probably only very slowly.

Some people still insist on entertaining the self-deceiving thought that thinking is being aware. Practicing the exercises you have been given, will be starting to demonstrate that you are more aware when you stop thinking. Thinking is a significant part of the illusion you are experiencing.

In the next chapter we will be looking at how to do Advanced Thinking. As Advanced Thinking requires very little, if any, thinking in the traditional sense, obviously your normal thinking process is actually an impediment or barrier to success.

So you have been encouraged to practice using the most essential ingredient to Advanced Thinking, your awareness. Have you been practicing enough ?

The answer for most people will be NO.

The desire to experience the illusion of Earht is so strong, that many people reading this book will hardly have practiced at all.

The illusion you are experiencing is designed to make you "want" to practice but, actually practice very little. Do not fight this force, as you will lose. Instead, be amused when you find yourself "wanting" to practice rather than actually practicing.

Seeing The Aura Illusion In Action

What you think you want

As previously mentioned, what you think you want and what you actually want are two entirely separate entities that can merge, but are frequently polar opposites. This book is designed to progressively make you more aware of what you actually desire, and less deceived by what you think you want.

Obviously, if you spend your life thinking you are trying to achieve something but actually you don't............ Do you think you could ever succeed ?

To give you access to genuine Free Will, it is clearly necessary that your human consciousness learns to recognise what you are creating. For example, would you let a one year old child steer the family car. As that one year old child would have little idea of what it was creating, what would be the likely outcome ?

In the last chapter you were practicing how to see your aura. Assuming you have actually been practicing this, one simple fact will have emerged. You often appear to be in the "wrong energy" for what you think you want to achieve.

For example, if you are trying to do lots of bright creative work, but your aura looks like a dark de-energising fog, do you really think you will succeed ?

Anyone who has done anything creative knows that, you need to be in the "right energy" to do it, otherwise the creativity does not flow, and you do nothing. Experienced or professional creative workers such as writers or artists know that when a creative wave of energy arrives, you should ride it for as long as you can; for it might not be there later.

By practicing looking at your aura you can see if you are in the "right energy" to do something, or not. By looking at other people's auras you can see if they are in the "right energy". This is a great management tool, as you can instantly tell who is capable of performing and who is not.

The essential point is to start to recognise that, whilst you will often think you want to do something, the state of your aura suggests that actually you don't. By making this sort of basic observation, you can become more aware of your actual desires.

So to be pragmatic and practical, instead of paying attention to what you think you want, why not instead just notice your aura and the energy you are radiating ? Then you will know what you wanted. Similarly, apply the same reasoning to what other people might want; look at the energy in their auras.

It will also benefit you to notice how thinking you want something while actually wanting another has some specific advantages. Take the example of physical death. This is the extraction system that gets you out of The Great Simulator Earht plane. Whilst the typical person you might meet in The Great Simulator Earht plane appears to be waiting to die, that same person will be humanly afraid to. So human beings are programmed to resist killing themselves (for obvious reasons), but ultimately it is necessary to remove them from the Earht plane.

Humour

Taking yourself, the human entity, seriously makes the illusion stronger. Recognising the "joke", of trying to do something whilst actually not wanting to succeed at all, is a great way to counteract this.

For example, take something you are trying to succeed at. Think about what it is. When you get to the end of this chapter, there is an exercise to help you recognise if you really want to succeed with that project, at this point in time. Many people will discover that actually they do not. At this point everyone tends to make the same mistake as follows:

- You look at your aura.
- Often it is not the way you think it should be.
- You do not see it as perfection.
- You use your thoughts to change it, to something you think you prefer.

Personally, I have spent years doing this. So I can bear personal testimony that trying to change your aura because you do not like what you find, is ultimately a waste of time. It's a bit like drinking coffee to be more alert and awake; you can get a short term boost but, ultimately, you end up no brighter, than you would be without any coffee.

Taking the state of your aura too seriously, blocks you from recognising the perfection of why it was that way to begin with.

To advance, you need to practice seeing the "joke" of what is happening. The alternative is to take everything too seriously which "sucks" you into the very thing you wanted to change in the first place.

Now, notice how whilst your aura is frequently in the "wrong energy" for what you think you want to do or achieve; it is, conversely, actually in the "right" energy to get you to pay attention.

Observe

Example, most people I know take the view that they want to be wealthier. People are normally as wealthy as their aura suggests, given a short space of time. So a wealthy person will have a wealthy aura. If you saw someone who had a wealthy aura, but they were currently poor, then you would know that was about to change. Conversely, if you saw a wealthy person with a poor aura, you would know that that person was about to lose a great deal of money.

In case you are wondering what a wealthy aura looks like, try looking for yourself at other people, in particular, look out for the brown colours and some creative energies and patterns.

Keep practicing observing auras and the physical reality of the situation.

Apply humour

You will have a strong desire to change things that are probably perfect. So, what is there to laugh at ? If you are trying to do something and the energy in your aura is dictating "No chance", you are likely to get upset.

Getting upset makes the illusion stronger. So the illusion is then harder to change.

A simple practical example is the emotion of fear. Fear is useful in that it encourages you not to kill your human body. It can also be a hindrance that makes you shy and afraid to, for example, introducing yourself to someone you would like to meet.

Remember that, an illusion is basically a situation which is the opposite of what it appears to be. Illusions are energised by you taking them seriously, this is because taking something seriously is "wanting to believe it".

When you use you sense of humour you are, simultaneously, recognising that you are "playing with reality".

Instead of wishing your aura was better suited to what you might be trying to accomplish, laugh at how it might not appear to be in the "right energy" to accomplish the thing you think you want.

You will require this humorous change of attitude to achieve fundamental changes.

Be aware

Practice these simple awareness exercises. Notice when you are seeing the "funny side", or taking yourself seriously.

The more you feel you need to be insightful, the more you need your humour. Otherwise, when you take yourself seriously, you will remain locked in the identity of the being that is creating the original problem or challenge.

As you can practice this by being aware of other people, here is an example of a situation you may encounter. Suppose someone was trying to be the best parent. This parent would tell you all the things they were doing to benefit and develop their child. However, a moment's awareness would reveal a simple truth; trying to be the best parent is NOT BEING the best parent.

So the energy, and hence the aura, of trying to be something is also the energy and aura of not being it. In this case you would find that the aura contained "caring energies", but it would also contain "frustrated and upset energies", which would make it hard to be a "perfect" parent.

You can, similarly, also practice noticing how often you tell yourself you are trying to accomplish something. Then notice how your aura displays an energy that makes success look difficult or unlikely. If you find this funny, it will probably change. But, if you became serious and just try to change it, your success will tend to be brief.

Equally, become aware of how auras can be perfectly aligned to what a person thinks he or she is doing; you can learn to recognise this through the physical success that results.

Energies and auras change quickly

When you observe energies and auras (they are really the same thing), you will also notice how quickly they can alter. This is a natural process that never stops.

You will have seen people's moods change, therefore practice seeing how their aura changes at the same time. With practice you will notice that an aura will usually change before a person says something or takes action.

When I am working with clients, and hence very alert, I often see how an aura changes as a person thinks; it goes brighter or darker faster that a human being can physically respond.

Humour helps auras change, whereas not liking what you find, getting upset and serious tends to delay changes. If you are practicing seeing or sensing auras, you will discover this is true.

This is why forcing your aura to be a particular colour, etc, is a waste of time, as soon you stop concentrating it changes.

What if you think you still can't see auras ?

Everyone can see an aura if they just let themselves do so. You might think that I am in a state of permanently recognising these things. But I don't. You could say that I am switching the ability "on and off".

Furthermore, the extent to which I see auras is often fleeting or only for brief moments, yet by simply paying attention, great insights can regularly be gained. So you can make significant advances if you just pay a little more attention.

In the event that you are having difficulty, here is a quick summary of how to see auras:

1. Remember that everything you can physically see is actually viewed using the same senses that give you your imagination. Seeing reality simply involves getting the special effects team to be quiet.

2. The Astral World is essentially not like Earht. The energy forms of the Astral have no need to conform to Earht normalities. What you see at an Astral Level, such as an aura, will appear different to Earht reality.

3. Just look at someone and remember that an aura is probably there. Now, let yourself receive impressions of whatever aura you think might be present. Let your impressions superimpose themselves on your image of that person; i.e. two images; physical and Astral of that person simultaneously.

4. Keep comparing your impression of what a person's aura looks like, versus how they feel and behave, etc. After a while, you will get very good at matching your impressions to their actual physical state.

5. Notice that when you are practicing, your guiding spirits are assisting you. They will give you a better sense, and some helpful interpretations of what you are seeing. For example, you might suddenly notice that you "know" what you are looking at, even though you will have had no prior experience of what it is you have just seen.

Basically you just stop telling yourself you can't see an aura and simply start noticing you can. To understand what they mean, keep comparing what you see and sense with Earht reality. After a while you will find that you can see and you know what you are seeing.

Another technique

If you look at any living thing, you will see a glow of energy around it. Some of the aura's "frequency" or "vibration" is so close to the physical world, you can generally see something in favourable light conditions.

Basically, you look for an outline of light around a body or a limb such as a hand, however, you might also develop a fixation with trying to "physically" see an aura. In that case you will have extreme difficulty in recognising the less physical aspects.

Seeing The Spirit Generated Illusion In Action

Auras are only half the story. The energy of an aura is created by a multitude of spirit beings. A human being will tend to believe that he or she is creating an aura, whereas, it is actually the other way round. Spirit beings combine their energies to create the impression that human beings exist. A human being's aura is actually composed of a multitude of spirit beings.

To understand why human beings behave the way they do it is, therefore, helpful to understand what the spirit beings, generating the illusion, are doing. Furthermore, the spirit beings are doing precisely what you, the super-consciousness, instructed them to do. You can determine a great deal about a human being's character, simply, by observing the characteristics of the spirit beings comprising its aura.

Simple observations you can make

This human belief system will initially incline you not to notice the greater reality around you. For example, you might think that an aura, such as, electricity, is not alive. The greater reality is that this energy is very much alive, and conversely, in the greater reality of matters, it is you the human that is not.
Ha ha.

Another typical confusion stems from an assumption that living things have form and, where appropriate, have personality; form and personality, in the human or animal sense, are actually inventions.

Your physical form (your human body) is an impression you have that does not actually exist. You are just experiencing a strong sense that it is there. You are actually an "energy entity" which has the impression that it is experiencing human form.

Your sense of being alive stems from the energy sensations you are experiencing.

Ultimately, there is only one being and you are it, but what you are experiencing, right now, is not you. It is, in fact, constructed from an amalgamation of spirit forms. What you, the super-consciousness actually want is manifested through these various spirit forms. Your guides are there to help you be more aware, whilst the lower beings are there to create the illusions.

To help you recognise what is happening here are a few reminders of things you can practice:

1. Human beings tend to think they are the sum of their thoughts. Using the exercise previously given, "Switch off this noise".

2. Feel the energy of your aura. Notice how it is giving you the impression of being alive.

3. Become more aware of how the lower beings give the impression that your aura is moving and changing independently.

A significant part of your human experience is a flood of thoughts and feelings. You will normally find that your head is filled with a variety of thoughts, feelings, images, voices (normally appearing to be your own). Previously, in Chapter 18, you should have practiced seeing the Special Effects Team in action. Now it is time to apply that skill.

If necessary, go back and practice how to notice the lower beings.

Summary of the connection between spirit beings and your aura

Your aura is an energy form. The lower beings or Special Effects Team are energy forms. Your consciousness is constructed from energy forms. Ultimately, they are all the same thing.

Hence, if you look at a person's aura, you can tell what is going on. You can see how a person's aura is constructed from lots of individual living entities.

As personalities tend to manifest physical shape of some sort, when you look at an aura you can see that it appears to be constructed from "lots of people (spirits)", though, as they are so mixed together, it normally looks more like a swirl of colours.

If you stripped away all the spirit entities, and their accompanying personalities, we would end up with your "essence". This has no real personality that a human being would relate to it, which is one of the reasons why a human consciousness does not easily recognise what it actually is. Everything that makes you feel alive, is derived from your sense of being a person. However, from an Astral perspective, what you really are, initially, appears to be a "nothingness".

To solve this basic difficulty, in recognising what you actually are, at this moment you are being helped to recognise what you are doing. In this particular case, we are looking at what the spirit beings, which compose your human consciousness, are doing. Furthermore, as you progress, you will recognise that they are doing precisely what you instructed them to do.

See a contradiction

For the purposes of developing your ability, this book will often focus on solving problems, or difficulties. Problems make you pay attention; good fortune usually sends most people to sleep.

You can, specifically, become alert to the following contradiction:

In your head you may think or desire that you want to do something.
Meanwhile, you are often controlled by feelings not to do it.

You may find this statement repeated a great deal and, there is a good reason. Your brain has been programmed not to notice this process, unless you access your higher awareness. As this takes a great deal of practice, you need repeated reminders; otherwise you will practice far less.

The Special Effects Team of spirit beings work virtually tirelessly for your benefit to achieve the illusion of the Earht plane. They even work when you are physically asleep at night. Under normal conditions, without accessing your higher awareness, their work will be undetectable. However, it is possible to detect their activities, through the anomalies or apparent contradictions in life.

Notice how frequently you think that you need to do something such as:

- Say hello to a neighbour.
- Start a pension.
- Tidy a room.
- Write a letter.
- Change your job.

How often have you found that you do not have the "energy" or "inclination" to do one of these sorts of things ? Instead, you find yourself wishing that you could do it but, actually, feel unable. In these cases, it is not that you are physically incapable, rather you will find that, somehow, you don't want to.

At this point most people start feeling less "good" about themselves. The conflict between feeling and thinking that there is something they should do, and not having the inclination or enthusiasm to do it, makes them frustrated and, often depressed.

Now at a higher level, this is precisely what you wanted to happen. Whilst at a lower level it will appear to be something you could never desire. This phenomenon can only be achieved on the Earht plane with the assistance of the Special Effects Team.

If you pay attention you will be able to see or sense the lower beings / Special Effects Team creating this effect. Practice observing them and notice the wonderful contradiction between what you say you want, and what, at a higher level you actually want.

Don't fight

When you observe yourself actually not wanting to do the very thing you thought you wanted to do, the natural reaction is for you to try and overcome your obstacle. However, that would be to deny the merits of why, at a higher level you instructed the Special Effects Team to block you, in the first place. So, even if you win a battle, this can be a war of attrition. If you fight at the lower level of what you think you want, you are likely to ultimately lose.

The lower beings that make up your Special Effects Team are expert in distracting, diverting and de-motivating you. They are energised by you at a higher level and, consequently, have a considerable advantage. Even worse, any desire to do battle with them will, of course, be what they want you to do, because they supply all of your thoughts and feelings. You would be acting without any Free Will so, viewed "from above", any combat would look pointless, absurd, and very amusing.

The simple alternative suggestion being offered to you is:

- Observe them in action.
- Congratulate them for their amazingly effective work.
- Practice being more self-aware.
- See the perfection.

Seeing a perfection

This is something that, initially, almost every human consciousness resists, denies and generally refuses to accept but, when you do see it, you will laugh, smile and often shed a happy tear or two.

When you take a warm loving approach to activities of the Special Effects Team, doing so simultaneously connects you to the wisdom of your guiding spirits, you become more aware.

Exercise To See What You Actually Want

Seeing yourself

The purpose of a human consciousness is to be able to see the real you. Actually the human consciousness can do this by literally looking, Astrally, through the top of its human head. When it does this, it will normally see the real you.

Generally, your human consciousness, only pays attention to the real you, when it is trying to solve a problem. If you give it lots of problems it will, often reluctantly, pay more attention, as opposed to rarely, if at all.

When a human consciousness "looks" through the top of its head, it will "see" the real you or super-consciousness. This rule has a simple exception. Sometimes a human consciousness appears to be so "out of alignment", that the real you, or super-consciousness, can appear to be off to one side. However, you are always there..... somewhere.

Fortunately, as soon as a human consciousness sees the real you, the super-consciousness, recognising and connecting to this light automatically corrects any apparent "miss-alignment". So the light of you, the super-consciousness, will no longer appear to be off to one side, but in its rightful place, directly above.

Exercise

Follow this exercise **as precisely as possible**. It causes your awareness to shift from thinking you are a human consciousness to recognising you are a super-consciousness, and back again.

When it is done with humour and love it works very well. If you, initially, do it to try and achieve some sort of "human endeavour", or resolve a problem, it tends to go wrong. Later, with practice, you will able to apply it to problem solving, but not yet.

The following procedure will give you, the human consciousness, a glimpse of what you really are, a super consciousness. Hence you will start to see what you actually want, as opposed to what you, in your human consciousness condition, think you want.

This can be intellectually difficult to understand, at first. The only way forward is to practice the following steps, until what has been written starts to make perfect sense:

1. Start from the perspective of being a human consciousness.

2. Take some issue that you currently have to resolve. For example, it could be a problem that upsets you and appears to have no simple solution.

3. Now try looking through the top of your head to see the light that is actually you.

4. If you don't see the light, it will be to one side or, in a severe case, below you. With practice it will, normally, appear to be exactly over your head, but that will sometimes, not be the case to begin with.

5. When you see the light, provided you don't insist on it being something entirely separate, you become it.

6. Recognising that "the light is me" generally helps. Look at it and become it with the recognition of "that's me".

7. Allowing yourself to become the light, briefly, requires no effort at all, but don't try to stay being the light for too long, as you will only become bored.

8. The next thing you will find is that you are a human consciousness again, but now more energised and aware.

9. If you are not that energised, repeat this process.

10. When you do feel more energised, then "look Down".

11. See the human form and its associated energies.

12. If possible, try to glimpse the Special Effects Team in action.

13. Observe the situations and challenges you are creating (through the Special Effects Team) for that human form below.

14. A FUNDAMENTAL ERROR is to try and fix anything at this stage. Just observe.

15. You need to see how you are creating, and perpetuating, the original problem or challenge.

16. A FUNDAMENTAL SUCCESS is to see yourself creating something that your normal human consciousness would never choose to do. Sometimes what you want and your consciousness think it wants are the same things, however, when they are complete opposites, recognising this is highly insightful.

17. If you do this exercise correctly it will make you laugh and, perhaps, cry with joy.

18. If you do this exercise correctly you will recognise the value in creating the original problem in the first place.

As long as you continue to recognise that value, you have no further need of that problem, or anything similar.

At this stage you may start to recognise spirit beings creating the Earht plane scenarios for you. If you do, then "well done", but if you do not, that is quite normal. Doing this exercise successfully generally requires repeated practice.

Practice this exercise plenty of times. Remember, it is not about solving problems, but recognising that you actually wanted them in the first place. Curiously when you do that you will instantly see practical solutions to the original problem. Your human consciousness will also experience the energy and inclination to act differently.

Welcome to the world of Advanced Thinking.

Question for the reader:
Did you manage to read this chapter and do the exercise with a clear and bright mind ?

If you did then carry on to the next chapter.

But, if you got drowsy, apathetic, or otherwise distracted, you should read it again !

23 Advanced Thinking

Thinking Versus Awareness

When you have clearly and consciously experienced both, the difference is obvious. You could say the difference is like "night and day".

You will have already experienced both, but you may not be recognising the difference. If you have been practicing the exercises in this book, you will understand everything you are about to read. Conversely, if what you are about to read does not make sense, then that is an indication that you need to practice more.

How Advanced Thinking Works

A human consciousness is constructed from a multitude of spirit forms. Most are actively helping you experience an illusion. This is what distinguishes your Guides from all the rest, for they are there to enlighten your human consciousness and lift you from the illusion.

If your human consciousness pays attention, your Guides can make it aware of things it previously never knew. No "working something out" is necessary, henceforward; traditional thinking is replaced with higher awareness.

What is Awareness ?

As we just recognised, it is a simple knowing. You do not have to "work anything out", as you will find that you already know the answers. Some people would define it as tapping into a "universal consciousness", where more or less anything can be known.

A human consciousness will experience limitations in knowing, or being aware of, everything as it tends only to be intellectually capable of doing one conscious thing at a time. Note that a human consciousness is highly capable of doing multiple *unconscious* things at the same time. But then, it is not conscious, is it ?

Here are a few suggestions to help you recognise what awareness is:

- Instant knowing
- A combination of seeing and sensing.
- Non-judgmental
- Matter of fact

No calculation or contemplation is required.

What is Normal Thinking ?

Memory

Instead of sensing the world around you as it is, you recall a memory of it. So if someone said something to you like "hello", you would recall a memory of having heard "hello".

The essential difference between thinking and awareness is that when you think you are always recalling a past impression of some sort. In this situation, you are not noticing or being aware of what is around you, instead, you are imagining it; you are not really in the "now".

Because thinking relies on memories as opposed to actuality, it can easily be full of errors. For example, how often have you read something quickly, only to find you had read it incorrectly ? In this case your memory would contain and perpetuate errors.

Disregard

One of the wonderful aspects of thinking is that it enables us to believe complete fantasies.

When you think you, normally, attempt to get the information at your disposal to fit into a logical pattern. Say you wanted to put the following numbers into a logical pattern:

6, 2, 10, 7, 4, 8.

A logical sequence that results could be:

2, 4, 6, 7, 8, 10.

But then if the 7 looked out of place you might be tempted to disregard it and the sequence now becomes.

2, 4, 6, 8, 10.

And forget that the 7 even existed.

When you think, you actively disregard information until whatever remains forms a nice logical pattern. Furthermore, as your thinking is determined by your feelings, what you choose to disregard is not governed by any real logic.

Therefore, if you want to believe something, you can easily do so, by disregarding the inconvenient facts and taking comfort in focusing on the remaining incomplete information that supports the belief you desire. This is how you have fantasies.

Calculation

There will often be facts you want to know but do not appear to. So you take the existing information at your disposal, disregard anything which appears irrelevant, and arrive at an apparently logical conclusion.

Now if the calculation is to add up the following numbers: 2, 4.

You get an answer of: 2 + 4 = 6

But if the numbers to add up were: 2, 4, 7,

and for whatever reason you again chose to disregard the 7,

then you still get an answer of: 2 + 4 = 6

and not the real answer of: 2 + 4 + 7 = 13.

When a human consciousness tries to work things out, its habit of disregarding information tends to produce inaccurate or corrupt answers.

The essential point is not that thinking is "bad", after all, it is an amazing capability, instead you should recognise that it has both advantages and disadvantages.

The Effect Of Normal Thinking

Believing you are a human being and not an integral part of a super-consciousness is made possible by thinking. As you wanted to experience life as a human being, thinking is an essential element in achieving this objective. The human power of rational thought is what sets a human being aside from most of the animal species.

When a human consciousness is dreaming at night, or experiences the transition of bodily death, it loses its ability to manifest rational thought. It loses its ability to order information and make calculations, instead it, has to rely upon its awareness and memories.

It is helpful if you can remember what it is like to function with the limited awareness of a dream state. In such a condition you will find you are not separate from your surroundings but, instead, tend to merge with them.

Normal thinking allows you to experience the world as a separate entity from everything around you, allowing you to be detached and aloof. This corrupts your awareness, but also makes something amazing possible.

It allows you to ultimately see and experience what you really are. The ability to experience your true self, the super-consciousness, from a different perspective is actually why you have given your human body the ability to think, in the first place, even though it may take many lifetimes to achieve this.

Advanced Thinking

Advanced Thinking is using your awareness and thought process without disregarding information.

This is only possible whilst experiencing human form, clearly you cannot, after all, do it when your body is dead or has not yet been born. The absence of a physical brain makes it impossible.

The typical reader of this book has developed his or her intellectual thinking skills. To enable you to consciously manifest some advanced thinking, simply requires developing your awareness skills.

At this very moment, your thinking process makes you believe that to some extent you are alive on Earht. This is despite the fact that your awareness is, simultaneously, recognising that you are not.

You disregard your sense of not being human, because you want to experience life in human form. If you have been paying attention, you will have noticed that you actually think, more or less, whatever you want regardless of logic, or of any greater reality.

Next step

You can't just suddenly become aware of everything. Your human brain has to learn how to process all the information. Higher Awareness, or Advanced Thinking, requires that you do not become too focused. However, when you learn a new skill you tend to focus, which causes you to disregard and ignore = not being aware.

You resolve this difficulty by letting your energy system "flow".

Here is a simple exercise that should help you recognise the difference:

1. Become aware of the energy flowing through your physical form.

2. Notice how it "flows" better when you breathe properly.

3. Now think about something. Concentrating your mind in the process.

4. Notice how this causes you to restrict your breathing and become *focused* in your head.

5. Restore your breathing and allow yourself to become *aware* of your body sensations and energy flows again.

Doing this exercise should help you recognise the difference between being aware and being focused; the two states *feel* entirely different.

Thinking and flowing

Assuming you are sitting (if not this will work equally well standing), use the last exercise to become more aware of the energies flowing through your physical form.

Observe how when you start to think you tend to become less aware, so thinking about something will make you less aware. However, because you are now less aware, you will not notice that you have become less aware. Instead, you will be happily engaged in contemplating your thoughts.

If you are not sure what the last paragraph means, just sit (or stand), for a moment, and notice how this is obvious when you pay attention. Thinking reduces your awareness, but as you now have a reduced awareness, you tend not to notice that you are less aware.

If thinking tends to reduce your energy flow, and make you less aware, clearly this is going to make thinking, whilst being more aware, difficult. Especially as, when you are thinking, you can easily be under the false impression that you are more aware.

Insight

The basic "problem" you are experiencing with thinking is that it tends to make you "introverted" or turn "inwards". Hence you focus on a limited set of senses and do not notice the greater reality around you.

Try training yourself to simply notice the greater reality, or world around you, without contemplating it.

At first, this is difficult because you behave as if you are the only one truly alive. So instead of tending towards aloofness, try connecting with the energy of what you observe, or are aware of.

For example, if you are near something as commonplace as a table, you tend to ignore that it, in its own way, possesses a rudimentary awareness and energy but, if you connect with this energy, it helps you to become less "introverted".

Tables will, quickly, fail to satisfy your interest for new things. You will probably find plants, animals and other human beings more interesting. Do practice this and see the difference.

To make Advanced Thinking easier, you therefore have to solve the challenge of not getting bored and introverted. The insight is that if you connect to the energy of a stone, or even the air around your human form, this stops you becoming introverted.

This should be a pleasure

Let's make this very simple. If you are not enjoying the experience of connecting to the energy of the things around you then you will become introverted. You will not enjoy what you are doing and, instead, return to contemplating thoughts and imagining things. In this case there won't be much Advanced Thinking going on.

To make the experience more pleasurable, here is a simple tip. When you breathe properly and allow your fingers and toes to connect with the Earht you will find that connecting with most things soon becomes a pleasure.

So instead of pushing yourself to connect with everything more, which no doubt some people will try, let's take an alternative approach of enjoying the connection with the Earht.

If you want to amuse yourself, notice the lengths you go to in order to stay "disconnected". You will then be able to observe one of the techniques you have been employing to block your Advanced Thinking.

Notice how, by jamming your breathing, it becomes unpleasant to connect to the energies of the things around you. If you relaxed your breathing it becomes easy. So amuse yourself by blocking your breathing, after all, you have already previously blocked it a great deal. By practicing blocking yourself, you will become more aware and actually block yourself less.

Doing this reverse exercise correctly will make you laugh.

Spirit World

Guides

Under normal conditions you, the human consciousness, will tend to believe that you are sitting or standing, etc, in a room…… whatever.

Your Guides are not under this illusion. They are aware that you are not really in that room on Earht at all (or wherever you are reading this book). They are aware that you just think you are.

Incidentally, when your body physically dies, they have to "wake you up" so that you start paying attention to where you actually are. Whenever you recall previous incarnation deaths, you will find your Guides are waiting for you so that they can help you with this necessary awakening.

So in physical terms, you could say that your Guides are around you, all of the time, whatever you are doing.

To sense their good company more easily, breathe properly and connect with the Earht, then let yourself enjoy the pleasure of connecting with the energy of your Guides.

Instead of spending your time thinking in an introverted state, practice and enjoy experiencing the energies of your Guides.

Special Effects Team

Whilst your Guides help you to be more aware, the Special Effects Team have the opposite role to perform......... Most of the time.

Your Special Effects Team are there to help you experience the limitations and illusions of normal thinking.

They are expert in helping you concentrate and limit your awareness.

So for you to experience Advanced Thinking, you need to become more aware of your Guides, and less diverted by the activities of the Special Effects Team.

However, achieving this requires becoming more consciously aware of the Special Effects Team. Whenever you do this, with an attitude of unconditional love and congratulation, they quieten and you can then easily connect with your Guides.

Exercise For Basic Advanced Thinking

As Advanced Thinking is something that you need to practice, all the exercises are designed to be simple and incremental so that anyone who truly pays attention will be able to do this.

At the end of the last chapter, the exercise was to connect with the light above your head that is really you. Repeat the same exercise, but this time, apply the insights and new skills you should have gained from this chapter.

Exercise

Follow this exercise **as precisely as possible**. It causes your awareness to shift from thinking you are a human consciousness, to recognising you are a super-consciousness, and back again.

When it is done with humour and love, it works very well. If you do it to try and achieve some sort of "human endeavour", or resolve a problem, it tends to go wrong.

The following procedure will give you, the human consciousness, a glimpse of what you really are, a super-consciousness. You will start to see what you actually want, as opposed to what you, in your human consciousness condition think you want.

As this can be intellectually difficult to recognise, even though you may think you know what you are looking for, practice the following steps until what has been written starts to make perfect sense:

1. Start from the perspective of being a human consciousness.

2. Take some issue that you currently have to resolve. For example, it could be a problem that upsets you and appears to have no simple solution.

3. Now try looking through the top of your head to see the light that is actually you.

4. If you don't see the light, it will be to one side, or in a severe case, below you. With practice it will normally appear to be exactly over your head.

5. When you see the light, provided you don't insist on it being something entirely separate, you become it.

6. Recognising that "the light is me", generally helps.

7. Allow yourself to become the light. Don't try to stay being the light for too long, as you will only become bored.

8. The next thing you will find is that you are a human consciousness again, but now more energised.

9. If you are not that energised, repeat this process.

10. When you do feel more energised, then "look Down" at your human form below.

11. Notice what you are creating below.

12. A FUNDAMENTAL ERROR is to try and fix anything at this stage. Just observe.

13. You need to see how you are creating and perpetuating the original problem.

14. A FUNDAMENTAL SUCCESS is to see yourself creating something that your normal human consciousness would never choose to do. Sometimes, what you want and what your consciousness think it wants are the same things. However, when they are complete opposites, recognising this is highly insightful.

15. If you do this exercise correctly it will make you laugh, and perhaps cry with joy.

16. At this point it is very easy to recognise the presence of your Guides.

17. By connecting to their unconditional loving energies, you will instantly experience a higher awareness.

18. If you do this exercise correctly you will recognise the value in creating the original problem in the first place.

As long as you continue to recognise that value, you have no further need of that problem or anything similar = **Problem solved**

Doing this same exercise, but enjoying the connection with everything, will start to make you recognise that a wonderful perfection exists. In an amusing way, things that you previously considered to be "problems" become redefined as desirable adventures.

Don't try to solve problems

Doing this exercise correctly will make you aware of the excellent reasons why problems are created in the first place. When you have made as much use of a problem as you need, then you will have no further need to create that problem.

Recognise the difference between Advanced and Traditional Thinking

When you are using the awareness of your Guides, you will experience a very different thought process. This exercise is an excellent way of discovering the difference.

Science Note

Practicing your Advance Thinking is also a fascinating way of observing the “Wonders of the Universe”. Here is a fundamental one that you can glimpse.

Albert Einstein described with incredible simplicity the relationship between energy and matter.

$$\mathbf{E = mc^2}$$

Energy = **Mass** times the **Speed of Light** squared

This equation describes what matter or mass is……. Energy.

The Earht plane appears to be constructed from mass or matter, whereas it is actually constructed from energy. Which is why, try as you might, you won’t be able to ultimately detect any matter, because it does not exist. It only appears to.

The essential difference between what is considered to be matter, and what is considered to be energy, is as follows:

Energy is moving around at the speed of light.

Whereas mass appears to be more static and hence “in one place”.

The Earht plane is a realm in which things appear to be separated; i.e. one thing not connected to another.

So you could (putting it crudely) say that matter is something that appears to exist when you make it appear to be separated from the speed of light.

By this simple means, the energy universe you experience yourself living in, on Earht, appears to be solid.

You are experiencing an amazing science experiment.

If you are practicing your Advanced Thinking exercises, this makes a wonderful illusion through which to observe through higher awareness. Something that Einstein experienced in order to achieve his understanding of the universe.

24 Love Yourself

If you want to see what is going on you have to appreciate and welcome, what you are creating.

Advanced Thinking Applied

One of the greatest barriers to successfully applying your Advanced Thinking ability is trying to work out a solution to a problem by thinking about it. Yet at that same moment you would believe that trying to work out the solution might produce the answer you need. Whilst this might be true for maths-related challenges, for most other applications you are fooling yourself; new solutions are normally the result of creative inspiration and not rational thought.

When you apply your Advanced Thinking you see what you are creating. When you are doing normal thinking, you experience the thought forms you have created. That is why, when you are doing normal thinking, you experience the problem happening to you.

Unbelievable

Initially, it appears to be a ridiculous proposition that you should want to experience a variety of hardships. There are so many examples of unpleasant, and apparently unwarranted, misfortunes that people go through, that the notion of these people really wanting to experience these difficulties can appear absurd.

Reality

The fact of the matter is that whatever you are experiencing on Earht is no more than a simulation. It's a simulation that appears very real, but it is not real.

The reason why the simulation appears so real is that you wanted to forget the greater reality. Earlier, we pointed out that the pleasure of watching a good film is completely ruined, by focusing on the fact that it is no more than an illusion. The pleasure you get from a good film, is derived from the emotions you experience, when you watch it. If you spend the whole time focusing on the fact it is an illusion, you become aloof and much of the pleasure is lost.

Alternatively, notice that you can enjoy a good film, whilst retaining a distant awareness that it is a film. You achieve this by blocking out your awareness of other things. For, example you would ignore that you were in the cinema, and you would ignore the fact that everything you were watching was contrived.

But what would happen if you never realised that the film you were enjoying was only a movie ? This book is here, to help you regain your greater awareness.

People like seeing films, because it brings them pleasure. You wanted to experience your human form, because it brings you pleasure. This book is here to remind you that you created the "storyline" and the "script". Most of all, regardless of what you may think, you are actually gaining a great deal of "fun and pleasure" from the Earht plane experience.

Love and Advanced Thinking

The fastest, and easiest, way to access your Advanced Thinking is to recognise that you wanted to experience this human life. If you want to block your Advanced Thinking, then see your life as an unpleasant imposition. Read this paragraph again.

Incidentally, save yourself some time. Trying to imagine that you wanted to experience some difficulty in order to access your Advanced Thinking does not work. You will experience a deep feeling of "resentment", that will overcome anything favourable you try to imagine. Plus, imagining anything is an inaccurate reconstruction of reality.

Let us observe a simple human characteristic, that you can use to your advantage. Human beings tend to do nice things to people they like, and unpleasant things to people they do not like. So you, a human conscious, will tend to assume that if something unpleasant is happening to you then, at some level, you don't like yourself.

Loving yourself more, with a sense of humour, makes it possible to access your Advanced Thinking ability. This approach makes it possible for you to enjoy any "defects", or "faults", that your human personality may appear to have. Because, by liking them, you give yourself permission to access your Advanced Thinking. You could say that loving yourself allows you to reward yourself.

Loving your "defects", or "faults", makes sense once you let go of the notion that a human personality was designed to be perfect. It is actually a perfect vehicle, or machine, that is designed to display apparent imperfections.

This is why you are constantly being reminded that you are simply experiencing an illusion. Illusions are more interesting, and made more exciting, by apparent imperfections or challenges.

To make the illusion more compelling you need strong forces that make you ignore the greater reality. Therefore, it is important that you experience some fear and anguish, otherwise it would be dull and boring.

Exciting things have, and will continue to occur. As it is you that is creating these events, for your own benefit, you could welcome and enjoy them. Loving them allows you to raise your awareness and, thereby, access your Advanced Thinking ability.

Simple technique

The following technique will work better and better each time you apply it. It creates a learnt reaction that will revolutionise your natural ability.

Remember….. No forcing yourself to be happy or loving.

Technique:

1. Recall those past challenges and problems that have, over a period of time, made you "smarter" and more capable.

2. Recall how you, ultimately, enjoyed developing yourself, even if it appeared to be "hard work" at the time.

3. Notice how you enjoy being challenged; it tends to make you feel more alive.

4. Notice how you do not always welcome challenges, when they arrive.

5. So now "re-programme" yourself to react to challenges, with the positive attitude you know you will have afterwards.

6. Learn to do this in under one second.

7. Success will feel like an uplifting energy boost.

8. At that moment you will have access to your Advanced Thinking ability. Use it.

Cosmic Joke

The illusion, that you are a human being, is made possible by your desire not to like the apparent imperfections of your human form. This dislike of your human form interferes with, amongst other things, your breathing. Consequently, you get preoccupied with thoughts, instead of using your awareness. Once preoccupied with what appear to be your thoughts, you can then find it difficult to recognise the joke you are playing on yourself.

To see through the illusion requires that you allow, amongst other things, your breathing to flow, then you will experience a far greater awareness. As you will tend not to like what you are, and restrict yourself, taking yourself seriously prevents you seeing the joke.

This belief that you are a human being alive on Earht requires that, to some extent, you must block your body's energy flows by blocking your breathing and engaging in lots of thinking. Thinking is, of course, one of the most vital components of the illusion you are experiencing. The resulting low level of awareness, enables you really, to believe that you are little more than a human being with, possibly, a spiritual aspect of some sort.

Notice how real and often serious life can appear to be.

Question

As believing you are alive on Earht requires that you block out a considerable amount of your unconditional love, is this what you want ?

Paradox / Possible Contradiction

To recognise what you really are requires that you love yourself.

For the simulation of human life to appear real, you must block out parts of this emotion.

For you to be reading this book required you to experience human form.

For the illusion of human form to be believable requires that you actively dislike yourself, to some extent.

And this book is here, reminding you to love yourself more !

Do you see the Cosmic Joke ?

Harnessing The Power

Most people tend to have an outlook on life that follows the following pattern:

- "I would be happier if I did not have ……………. problem."
- "My life would be better if I had more of the things I need, such as more money."

When it comes to actually solving these sorts of challenges and acquiring additional resources, such as more money, most people often experience a combination of frustration and lethargy. Furthermore, in order not to look too stupid, people have a tendency to apply themselves to courses of action that will never solve the original challenge. A human being will go to extraordinary lengths, pointlessly, pursuing a solution to a challenge, despite that particular approach being a complete waste of time.

Under your nose

All human consciousnesses experience distress in one form or another. A few examples would be:

- Feeling lonely.
- Pain.
- Lack of confidence.
- Frustration and irritation.

A typical human consciousness will try to get away from these unpleasant feelings. Examples of trying to escape such feelings would be:

- Daydreaming.
- Switching off and going into a sort of suspended animation.
- Becoming preoccupied with something of little relevance.

- Deliberately upsetting other people, so as to somehow distribute the original distress.

Now here is an insight you should try to remember:

The force you require to solve your original challenge is, quite literally, under you nose.

Instead of trying to run away from it............ Embrace it.

That feeling of distress, or emotional discomfort, you have been trying to avoid is actually there to help you.

If you do not harness the power to solve your challenge and, instead, try to avoid it, how do you expect to solve it ?

Unconditional love

Is how you love these forces.

In order to understand how you might apply more unconditional love let us look at the subject of Creative Visualisation.

Useless Creative Visualisation

Let's not get confused; Creative Visualisation is a very powerful tool and can be employed most successfully. Use it more.

Useless Creative Visualisation on the other hand is a completely different entity that should be recognised as such. Coal and diamonds are both made out of carbon. One makes a nice fire to keep you warm and the other helps women to look pretty, but you would not want to get them confused. Imagine trying to make a fire with a sack full of diamonds, or how would a woman react to being given a coal engagement ring ?

The simple difference

Creative Visualisation has to be linked to an energy, for "action" to get the required results.

Obviously then, Effective Creative Visualisation is a marriage between a good plan and the necessary physical energy to actualise it.

Conversely, Useless Creative Visualisation is where the plan has not been linked to the necessary physical energy to actualise it.

In fact, Successful Creative Visualisation could normally be accurately described as follows. You feel the energy for action. The energy inspires you with a visual plan of action. You carry out your plan using the energy for action. You succeed.

Why this disconnection occurs

At the risk of boring you with repetition, if you do not love the force that will actualise your plan, then the likelihood is that you will not employ it.

Alternatively, you might, under protest, employ the necessary force for action, only to then abandon it at your earliest convenience. Such an approach creates the strong likelihood of the original problem recurring; you have an abundance of lifetimes at your disposal, with ample opportunities, to prove this for yourself.

Be more aware of how the necessary force for action does not always appear pleasant when you first encounter it. Strangely, once you start employing it, it generally feels fine and, often, actually becomes pleasant.

A simple example you will have already experienced is as follows:

- Sometimes you don't want to do something.
- You resist starting.
- Once you get going you enjoy that activity.
- At that point you are enjoying and encouraging the necessary force for action.

The simple truth is that the energy to create physical action does not always feel pleasant, when you first encounter it. So, if you are visualising something you are trying to achieve, but do not like the feeling of the energy that achieves physical results, you will not tend to employ that energy. Not employing the energy for action is the simple definition of "daydreaming".

How to spot a this disconnection

There are numerous ways, but here is a simple observation you should be able to make.

Note that Effective Creative Visualisation is like driving a car. You focus on where you intend to go, and then simply steer in that direction.

Conversely, Useless Creative Visualisation does not appear to get you anywhere. So notice how often you are planning, or intending to do something, and it does not happen. Staying with the car analogy, it would be like turning the steering wheel of the car whilst it was NOT in motion. Your Creative

Visualisation would initially appear to be steering you in the right direction but, actually, it would be completely pointless.

How often do you attempt Creative Visualisation that is divorced from the energy to actualise your plan ?

Are you clear on the profound difference ?

If not, read this section on "Useless Creative Visualisation again.

Self-sabotage

Your human brain is a calculator. A very accurate calculator. It measures your intention to achieve something and calculates if you have connected to the required physical energy for success.

A simple example would be jumping over a puddle. Your brain calculates the energy required to jump over the puddle, and compares it to the energy available to make the leap. If you are not sufficiently energised, it recommends walking around the outside of the puddle, instead.

Where you can easily self-sabotage yourself is by disconnecting from the necessary energy for action. Your brain is a fantastic tool for assessing the viability of any plan but if, during the assessment process, a disconnection occurs between the necessary energy for action and the challenge ahead, then your brain will recommend inaction.

The thinking process tends to diminish unconditional love, hence it tends to reduce your connection to the energy for action. That is why, the more people think about something, the less likely they are to take action successfully. Unless, that is, they maintain the connection to the energy for action.

Everything Is Back-To-Front

As a human consciousness you will be inclined to get ideas, and start thinking about them. When you get an idea, you will tend to sense and visualise it. If there appears to be sufficient energy for action, then you turn the idea into an Earht reality.

So you might experience the idea that you wanted to be richer. You might then employ your visualisation skills to imagine having more money and possible ways of obtaining it. As we have just observed, if this desire to have more money is disconnected from the energy to get it, time spent visualising will not produce results.

A different perspective

You, the super-consciousness, want your human consciousness to pay attention to what you are. A simple way of encouraging this to occur is by setting your human consciousness various challenges, that can only be completed if it pays, at least a little, more attention. That is, pays more attention to what it actually is; i.e. an extension of you. The degree of additional attention might not be great, in respect of each challenge or even lifetime, but it does incrementally add up.

Take the "I need more money" idea. Most people reading this book will always have access to sufficient money to satisfy their basic needs. So the "I need more money" idea could be better described as an emotion of dissatisfaction; i.e. "I am not happy as I am, but I would be if I had more money."

If everyone who wanted more money received more, as soon as they thought of it, then most people would be incredibly rich. Whereas, what actually happens, in most cases is that people experience a feeling that they do not have enough money. This feeling turns into thoughts and then they start trying to work out how to solve their problem. Of course, that then disconnects them from the energy for action, and they get nowhere.

The feeling of "not having enough money" is, typically, an unpleasant experience. It is the sort you will want to escape by acquiring more money. However, the evidence all around you is that, no matter how much money you acquire, you can still experience that feeling. This is why instances of "greed" are so common.

The feeling of "not having enough money" can be turned into an energy for action that produces dramatic results. However, this new application of the feeling requires a healthy co-operation with it, in fact, the more of that feeling exists, the more productive you can potentially be.

As we just noticed, most people are trying to get away from that feeling. However, it was you, the super-consciousness, that wanted your human consciousness to experience it, in the first place. In this example it is you, the super-consciousness, which gives your human consciousness that feeling, for a simple reason; to get it to pay attention.

For a human consciousness it is impossible to be unconditionally loving to something it does not like, just because it "knows it has to". A human consciousness can only be unconditionally loving, to the "I don't have enough money", feeling when it connects better to you, the super-consciousness. By making a human consciousness experience the unpleasant feeling of "I need more money", ultimately, it has to pay attention. Otherwise, it will normally not succeed, that is how it has been designed.

Trying this for yourself, you will need to love yourself more, to break this cycle of thinking about how to solve a problem.

INSIGHT: It is also worth noting that most people actually get more money by providing a service of some sort. Therefore, in most cases, getting more money involves providing a better service, or providing a good service to more people. Similarly, loving yourself more involves loving others more. Do you see the win-win connection ?

Back-to-front world

Money is sometimes said to be "the cause of all evil". People's attempts to escape their feelings of not having enough of it cause all sorts of "greedy" behaviour, and account for a great deal of human suffering.

Yet you, the super-consciousness, want your human consciousnesses to experience this force. Your human consciousnesses cannot ultimately escape through getting more money, by whatever means. Your human consciousnesses can only react to this force, differently, by being progressively more loving towards it. To do that, they have to pay more attention to what they actually are.

So actually you, the super-consciousness, are the cause of global suffering. Through a wide variety of different ways, you give your human consciousnesses feelings they do not initially appreciate. Frequently, in their attempts to escape these feelings, they cause endless suffering to other human consciousnesses.

Ultimately, they pay attention and, gradually, instead of trying to avoid such feelings, they work with them to produce win-win results for all concerned.

Human consciousnesses get particularly confused when they start to think of you as either a vengeful, or benign, God. Whereas, you are really neither.

In the back-to-front world that is Earht, you have created an amazing playground where it is:

- Impossible to die (as human life is only an illusion to begin with).
- Impossible to escape (as there is no-where to go).

Loving Yourself More

Summary: For you - the human consciousness

- You can only demonstrate Advanced Thinking by using unconditional love.

- You can only solve your fundamental challenges by using unconditional love.

- You, the human consciousness, cannot escape the challenges that you, the super-consciousness, give yourself.

- You have all the time, and opportunities, you need, to discover how to pay attention in any situation. There is no need to hurry as there is an indefinite amount of time to achieve this.

How to love yourself more

If there is still any doubt as to how simple this is, then here are a few reminders:

- You are, actually, a being that is "overflowing" with unconditional love.

- In order for you, the human consciousness, to experience more unconditional love; just block it less.

- You will block it less whenever you remember what you actually are; a super-consciousness.

Important point of detail

Some people will experience the thought "I am a super-consciousness". At which point there is an important distinction to be aware of.

When you are *recognising* yourself as a super-consciousness, you experience a wonderful unconditional love and a great awareness. Even if you only achieve a very limited degree of recognition, you will experience, at least, an uplifting energy surge of unconditional love. Whenever you actually recognise what you are, you will experience a physical difference.

Conversely, it is very easy to think that you are a super-consciousness, and experience no more than being a human consciousness, deluding itself that it is a super-consciousness. Similarly, you could imagine yourself to be swimming but never enter the water or even get wet. It is very obvious if you are swimming as opposed to imaging you are swimming. Swimming has a distinctive physical sensation, and imagining swimming does not.

No book can guarantee that you will experience a distinctive physical sensation, this is something only you can do for yourself. However, this book would be incomplete if no clear guidance was given to you.

So, remain alert to the difference in physical sensation between recognising and imagining you are a super-consciousness.

Finally, when you are recognising that you are a super-consciousness, you will not think. Your human brain will process the awareness of what you are, but it will not be thinking, in the traditional sense. Thinking is the act of imagining things without experiencing them at that moment. Thinking is not "living in the NOW". So thinking that you are a super-consciousness is a definite indication that you are actually experiencing being a human consciousness.

Exercise

Take yourself less seriously

One of the reasons, why a human consciousness blocks out its abundant unconditional love, is that it does not like what it thinks it is. This may not initially be easy to change for the following simple reasons:

- You wanted to dislike your human form.
- This dislike is an essential part of the mechanism that makes your illusion of human form appear convincing and real.

So what you are going to do is release yourself, if only temporarily, from the confines of the human identity you are clinging to.

See your incredible success

The simple way in which a human consciousness manages to dislike itself is by thinking it is somehow not good enough. Let us just pick a few typical ways in which people manage to not like themselves:

- I am too fat.
- If I was cleverer I would earn more money.
- I don't like myself because "X (person)" does not like me.
- I do not feel happy.
- I do not like the way I am and wish I was different.

Essentially human consciousnesses lock them into identities they do not like and block the very energies they would require to succeed.

Instead of seeing this as a failure........
Why not instead see this as an incredible success.

After all, you are an amazing super-consciousness that has managed to create a convincing illusion that you are a human being. It's quite an achievement.

Step through a contradiction

You want to experience being a human being. The fact that you are reading this book is immediate proof that you are actively experiencing this illusion. Your desire to experience human form is more powerful than the apparent will of your human consciousness.

Yet, what you are in the process of doing is attempting to see through the illusion that you are actively creating. Therefore, you are trying to overcome a force that is more powerful than you, the human consciousness, are. Trying not to do something you actually want to do, is a great contradiction.

This will, and is designed to, remain an insoluble contradiction, unless you recognise the purpose of why you are experiencing being a human consciousness. You actually want to recognise the glory and magnificence of what you, the super-consciousness, really are. You want your human consciousness to pay attention.

Whenever you recognise what you are, the illusion, of thinking and believing you are a human being, lifts. It will reappear as soon as you stop. So you can, at least briefly, step through this contradiction.

Time for a great laugh

This is a direct extension of the exercise in the last chapter. So please re-familiarise yourself with it, if necessary, so that now we can focus on adding some refinements that will benefit you.

SUCCESS

Succeeding with this exercise can be measured by the following three things happening:

1. What you will recognise will make you laugh a great deal.
2. You feel warm and loving towards your human form.
3. Everything will appear to be perfect.

THE EXERCISE

Whilst practicing the exercise in the last chapter, here are the refinements to apply:

1. As before, breathe better and connect to the Earht.

2. As before, look up through the top of your head and see yourself.

3. As before, feel that energy surge in your human form.

4. As before, look down at the human experience you are creating.

5. Now see the incredible achievement you have created:
   - Recognise how effectively you allow your human form to block itself.
   - Recognise how effectively you let your human form believe it is less capable than it really is
   - Recognise how funny it all is.
   - Recognise the amazing perfection.
   - Love yourself.

6. Repeat the process from step 1.

So much of your human experience is dominated by a lingering sense of not being somehow good enough. It can be dominated by almost ceaseless activity, designed to enable you to avoid the "terrible" feeling of, somehow, not being good enough.

Doing this exercise correctly will enable you to enjoy the fantastic wonder of what you really are, and the human consciousness you are simultaneously experiencing. Have fun loving yourself.

There is NO intellectual substitute to doing this exercise. Thinking about it, and imagining it, does not produce the experience.

25 Free Will

Awareness

Most people reading this book will initially read this far without having substantially practiced their Advanced Thinking skills, to any significant degree. Much as you might try, you will not be able to imagine, accurately, what is being described here. You can only experience Advanced Thinking and recognise when you are actually demonstrating Free Will.

One of the amazing features of experiencing a human consciousness is that, as it becomes less aware, it tends not to recognise that it is, indeed, less aware.

In a highly aware state, it is obvious that you are experiencing a high awareness. Whilst in a state of low awareness, you will tend to think that you are still highly aware.

Notice the practical difference between the two states:

- When you *are* in a highly aware condition you are *aware* that you are aware.
- When you *are not* in a highly aware condition you often *think* that you are aware.

You can stop fooling yourself by becoming more alert to the physical difference between *thinking* you are self-aware and actually *being* self-aware:

- Thinking is being absorbed by introverted thought forms.
- Awareness is noticing and feeling the energy forms around you.

Being aware is accompanied by an unmistakable physical sensations.

The simple truth is that typical rational thought guarantees that you will be experiencing a very low level of self-awareness. You can think that you are being highly aware, but you are just fooling yourself.

Whenever you demonstrate a high level of awareness or self-awareness, in the end it's the same thing, you will know that what is written here is as accurate a description as could reasonably be expected. You will know.

Recognising My Free Will

This book was written to help you perform your one purpose and, in the process, demonstrate some Free Will. The two go hand in hand.

It is difficult to recognise what you are without, simultaneously, demonstrating some Free Will. Similarly, it is impossible to overcome the power of your Free Will unless you recognise what you are.

Whenever you believe you are a human being, you will experience life happening to you. You will not be able to demonstrate any Free Will, even though you appear to have freedom of action.

When you recognise what you are, you will similarly recognise the experience you are creating for your human forms or consciousnesses. You will recognise the perfection of what you are doing. You will never find anything imperfect or "wrong".

At this point, it is possible for you to change what is happening to your human forms, after all, you are creating it.

Now, to those human consciousnesses who have been following the training offered in this book, a simple fact should have emerged; a simple fact that decides whether or not you will experience any Free Will.

You can never change anything unless you recognise what you are creating in the first place.

Such a recognition is accompanied by an overwhelming sense of perfection.

An implication of this fact is that, if you permit yourself to recognise the incredible perfection that exists, you may not ultimately wish to change something you previously wished to alter.

Incidentally, one of the reasons why experiencing higher awareness can be an extraordinarily amusing experience is that you will spot the most incredible contradictions........... in action. The world really does look "back-to-front". And very funny.

Demonstrating Free Will

So let's recap. If you demonstrate sufficient awareness to achieve some Free Will, you will also be aware of the incredible degree of perfection that actually exists. Hence you may not want to change anything. So what is the point ?

When you are manifesting that degree of awareness, something else happens; something that allows you to manifest some Earthly Free Will. You will experience what you are creating from a different perspective, and understand what you are actually doing.

Life From A Different Perspective

The human experience only appears to exist so that you, the super-consciousness, can see yourself. It should be similarly recognised, that you are having some loving fun in the process. Everything you create is designed to fulfil that intention.

In many respects, the glory of what you are doing can be all the greater, when you increase the level of the challenge you are setting yourself.

You, the super-consciousness, could create a great prophet who would appear to walk the Earht. The prophet would be largely aware what he or she was. The prophet would be inclined to say things like "I am the son (or daughter) of God", which would be true of all human forms. However, seeing yourself, the super-consciousness, is relatively easy from the perspective of a highly aware prophet. More challenging, and perhaps more fun, is seeing yourself from the perspective of more humble or distracted individuals.

If you make life too difficult for one of your human consciousnesses, it may not have a moment to spare to pay attention. Similarly, if you make life too easy for it, then it might lack the inspiration and stimulation to want to pay attention.

I recently worked with a client who had, inadvertently, done a wonderful job of balancing his auric energies. He had an excellent quality of life and, overall, was very happy. However, at a higher level he hungered for more. In order to increase the challenge, he knowingly had to embrace some new "dark forces". Living in complete harmony can rapidly become boring and unfulfilling.

Evolved souls

Do not really exist as such, because all souls are, of course equal. Human consciousnesses, experiencing a spiritual orientation, have a tendency to want to think that they are "evolved", in some form or other. Who do they think they are fooling ?

Yet there is a phenomenon that human consciousnesses should be aware of, whilst there is not a linear link from one human incarnation to another, a human consciousness can utilise the experience of one life, in another. Any human consciousness can appear to be "evolved", by taking advantage of this linking mechanism. You can be incredibly more capable, and appear more evolved than other human beings, merely by drawing upon your experiences of other incarnations.

Furthermore, because everything is connected, any human consciousness is already connected and a part of every other soul and spiritual entity. So, if a human consciousness has a "problem", there is lots of potential help available.

Remember what you are

Many people try to take advantage of this mechanism, by praying for assistance in the Earhtly challenges they face. They might pray to God, a deceased relative, a prophet or saint of some sort, and even one of their previous incarnations, etc. A human consciousness could be "smarter", and fulfil its purpose more easily, by remembering what it is.

This is why seeing human existence from a different perspective is a vital stage in recognising the illusion.

To demonstrate higher awareness is not intellectually knowing that everything is connected, it is experiencing that there is only actually one of us. So, instead of a human consciousness praying, to some external entity, to solve its problems, it could take advantage of the fact that it is part of that entity.

Human Beings have no Free Will

For one thing they do not actually exist, so viewed "from above" it would be absurd if an illusion had Free Will. Anyway, there is only one Creator, so there is no actual conflict as to what is being created. This is because anything in The Great Simulator that experiences itself as separate from you, the super-consciousness, has also disconnected itself from the capability of you, the sole creator.

It's a remarkably simple system. However, the realisation that it actually has no Free Will does not necessarily assist the development of a human consciousness. It easily becomes amoral and inclined to attempt to harm other human beings. The challenge of demonstrating any Free Will can appear so vast, that a human consciousness will instead just follow any whim or feeling it experiences, in the certain knowledge that this is perfection. As such whims or feelings will, almost always, be inspired by lower beings of some sort, that human consciousness is bound to experience new difficulties and challenges.

So, the potentially impossible task, for a human consciousness to experience what it actually is, has been made compensatingly easy. The amount of Free Will that a human consciousness need demonstrate to resolve, even the most apparently impossible challenge, is generally very small. A brief moment's recognition of what it actually is turns a human consciousness into a creator. The resulting expression of Free Will can change almost anything.

With practice, a human consciousness can then attempt new challenges which require a greater degree of awareness. It's all a matter of moving out of the illusion and gaining a true perspective on how the Earht plane functions.

Seeing My Free Will In Action

Let's take a look at some practical situations that can only be resolved by accessing some degree of Free Will.

Alcoholism

This happens when some of the more "devious" members of the Special Effects Team dominate a human consciousness. These lower beings enjoy encouraging the energies that radiate from a human consciousness when it consumes alcohol.

The human consciousness will then tend to have the following experience:

- It will find that a strong force is dominating it.
- It will not like its behaviour.
- It will love itself less.

As the human consciousness loves itself less, it becomes easier for the lower spirit beings to control it.

For alcoholics who recover during that incarnation, in one form or another, they all recognise that they are part of something greater. When they do this, they access sufficient Free Will to "change" the instruction being given to the lower beings; something else gets created instead.

Drug addiction

Is similar to alcoholism. Again, the human consciousness has to recognise that it is more powerful than the spirit beings that previously controlled it.

Once the lower beings constructing the addiction get a new instruction from their creator, they stop. Take note; that is how the Special Effects Team operate.

Religious addiction

Setting aside the desire some human consciousnesses have to control other human beings through the use of religious institutions, this is a very common challenge.

All human consciousnesses will to some extent recognise that "something is not right". What they actually recognise is that they are not experiencing being their true self, the super-consciousness. Precisely how conscious they are as to the origin of this feeling varies, but the effect is the same; they want to "reconnect".

This feeling of separation is usually accompanied by a lack of fulfilment with the rest of their Earht lives.

Normally, there is also some sense that God, or something similar, can solve their Earhtly problems, if approached correctly.

Anyway, they feed the addiction by worshipping and serving God, in whatever form they believe appropriate. What such human consciousnesses rarely recognise is that they take their worshipping and service so seriously that they are, systematically, blocking their higher awareness.

This addiction is normally sustained by a failure to recognise that a very highly entertaining illusion is occurring. Therein lies a cure for most of these addicts; to access Free Will normally requires humour.

Money addiction

This is a slightly contradictory description, as most money addicts are not that wealthy. However, the symptom they all suffer is a sense that they do not have enough money. Strangely, becoming wealthier does not appear to eliminate the symptoms.

Typical signs of this addiction are:

- Ever increasing need for money.
- Little or no concern for the adverse effect the accompanying behaviour has on other human beings.
- Money becomes an overriding goal.

One successful cure is the recognition that there is only "one of us", and they are part of it. Overcoming this perceived lack of resources is normally achieved by the recognition that there is more they could do to benefit their fellow human beings. Similarly, becoming wealthier at the expense of others, tends to delay their own consciousness's development.

By manifesting the Free Will to be of greater service to their fellow consciousnesses, these individuals tend to become more "successful". At which point, one way or another, they will end up with sufficient resources to meet their real needs.

Summary

Human beings face a multitude of challenges. It takes a minimal increase in their awareness, for them to recognise what they are and overcome these challenges.

Advancing The Different Perspective

This is where you get your human consciousness to demonstrate some Free Will by reducing the illusion.

Time

From a higher perspective it is clear that time does not exist. The simplest way of relating this to a human consciousness is to say that "moments" exist. To be slightly inaccurate but, at least, convey some sense of the greater reality, you could explain time as follows:

There is a great "mass", or collection, of different moments, all "pressed together". If you make them appear to be stretched out in a linear form (like a line), then you get the illusion of a time line. You, the super-consciousness, create as many moments as you want. You can also make them appear to go from a "ball" of time to being a "line" of time.

The human consciousness perceives itself to be in a realm (Earth), where these moments appear stretched out to create linear time. That is how time appears to exist on Earht.

When a human consciousness starts to recognise what it actually is, and exercises the option to experience some Free Will, the issue of time becomes critical.

One of the amazing features of the human brain is that it has a great capacity for dismissing, or ignoring, information. When it experiences the thought patterns that result from super-consciousness awareness, time appears as a mass of moments. Initially, a human brain will not comprehend this. The human form that is reading this book should be aware, that the brain has a tendency to ignore what it does not understand.

This means that, initially, when a human brain encounters time in its actual form and not the linear one it is used to, it will tend to ignore what it encounters. At the same moment that a brain is ignoring how linear time has ceased to exist, it will also be limiting its ability to demonstrate Free Will.

Effect of no time

This book is intended to help human consciousness manifest Free Will; to do that they have to "break out" of their old identities and recognise a greater reality. Whilst it is impossible to include all the relevant information in a book, it is possible to include a great deal of useful information. This book is like a map, intended to guide a human consciousness through unfamiliar terrain. It does not provide all the information, but it does provide essential directions.

Recognising moments, of time, in their original form is vital to experiencing yourself, as the super-consciousness you are. The human consciousness is inclined to believe that it is actually one person; whereas you designed it to knit together a multitude of personalities and produce the illusion of one single unified identity. It is truly an amazing illusion.

When the human consciousness is recognising what you are, and what it is, time ceases to exist. You can recognise where time would exist but, simultaneously, you recognise that it is just an illusion.

If a human consciousness believes linear time exists, then it is not really recognising that it is a part of you, the super-consciousness. Here you have another simple indicator of how aware you are being and, similarly, manifesting some Advanced Thinking.

Incidentally, for human beings with a comprehension of Einstein's Theory of Relativity, it is possible to glimpse some aspects of the relationship between time, matter and energy, but that doing so is not an essential part of the exercises in this book.

Fixing itself

When a human consciousness is experiencing human life it is continually trying to fix "things" and/or change what it perceives itself to be. Conversely, when it is experiencing what it actually is, it will recognise that the human form, it previously thought it was, was actually just a collection of interesting moments and personalities knitted together.

Nothing actually needs fixing.

Everything that appears to take place on Earht is just part of an ongoing creative process.

Doing Something Different

The false sense of time, a human consciousness will experience, is one of the simple means by which it achieves its sense of identity. In its sense of identity it continually perceives imperfection. This sense of imperfection is one of the "blocking energies" that enables the illusion of human life to appear real.

A human consciousness is programmed to constantly try to improve, or "fix, itself". Such activity prevents it from recognising what it actually is. Furthermore, such behaviour tends to make it want to re-experience, what it perceives as, previous moments where its identity appears to have performed poorly.

Put simply, if a human being experiences a problem, but is not happy about how it thinks it solved that problem, then it will try to recreate it. Thus, human beings find themselves continually trying to solve the same problems.

From a higher perspective, they are actually trying to stay in "previous moments".

If a human being would "let go" of these previous moments, then it could experience something new.

On a point of passing interest, Karma appears to exist because of this phenomenon. From one lifetime to another, a human consciousness can go through the motions of trying to resolve a series of challenges, or problems, in the form of "life lessons". So the very human beings who consider themselves to be "evolved souls", or whatever other complimentary term they ascribe to themselves, could equally be described as not really paying attention to the greater reality. As these "evolved souls" are particularly inclined to read this sort of book…….. Wake Up.

If a human consciousness recognised that it was none of the human identities it is designed to perceive itself as, then it would not need to "fix" any of them. Hence it could feel free to have some new experiences.

Recognising how the illusion of linear time links all these otherwise separate moments into a singular human identity is an essential part of manifesting your Free Will.

The Final Exercise
(In this book)

To be fair, from the perspective of a human consciousness that is trying to recognise what it is, following the exercises given in this book on your own could reasonably be described as "Not Easy".

To "get anywhere" there are basically two routes:

1. Get some proper training from a human being who knows how to do "this stuff".
2. Pay attention to the assistance offered by your Guides.

For quicker results, apply both approaches simultaneously.

The challenge all human consciousnesses face is, that even though they can read the instructions, their human heads will appear to be full of other thoughts and emotions. So whilst the directions might clearly say "go left", the human brain can ingeniously interpret this as "go right".

A human, or spiritual, guide can spot this happening in the moment. A human consciousness often does not.

The response of human consciousnesses to this challenge can veer it into either premature abandonment of the project, or fanaticism. Premature abandonment is where someone gives up relatively easily. Fanaticism is where someone is so obsessed with trying to do something perfectly and follows every instruction to the letter (including typing mistakes). Fanatics lose all sense of what they are actually doing.

So looking for a middle and sensible route, let human consciousnesses trying these exercises on their own follow this suggestion. The exercises and directions given are very precise and have been tested. They work. The typical mistake made, is to ignore parts of them.

Consider the exercises and directions as a skeleton. If you assemble this skeleton, as directed, you can easily mount the rest of the body you are creating on it. If you leave bits out, or substitute new erroneous components, then the rest of the puzzle will not fit and you will have to go back a few steps.

You have a good description of the steps, in the exercises.

You have a good description of the results you will experience, if successful.

If you do not appear to be experiencing the results described, just go back a few steps. The error is bound to be a simple one.

Experiment

Let us see if the human consciousness reading this can let go of something it is very attached to, and which it considers to be integral to its human identity.

Some readers will be hoping to resolve some problem, or challenge, they perceive. Master this exercise first, and then apply your skill to whatever you like. If you want to experience rapid progress, keep the "learning" steps easy. If you, the human consciousness, are desperate to solve a problem, or challenge, in your desperation you will be largely oblivious of how you are creating it. After the disappointment of failure, you will have to go back a few steps. Master this experiment, before applying it to your more exciting projects.

For different readers, there may be different examples. The thing to experiment with is letting go of what could in a humorous way be described as an "old friend". From the perspective of the Special Effects Team, it's an old team of friends.

Now take a moment to make a choice. The less of a "problem" or "challenge" you pick, the easier this experiment will be, then you can try some progressively harder ones.

NOW

What FEAR do you, the human consciousness, identify as part of yourself.

People like to define themselves as the sum of their perceived positive qualities. They also define themselves as the sum of their perceived negative qualities. Quite where the Fear you pick may fall, within these two categories does not really matter.

Pick a Fear that does not really matter. If you plan a rapid reunion with your super-consciousness, then pick your fear of standing in front of a moving car on a highway……. That was a Joke.

Pick a Fear that defines who you are inclined to think you are as a human being, but not one that is likely to have a negative effect on your human survival.

Here are a few examples that may be helpful:

- Fear of meeting new people (I think I am a shy person).
- Fear of appearing stupid (I always have to be the smartest person)
- Fear of commitment (I know I will change my mind in the next five minutes)
- Fear of technology (I cannot understand instruction manuals)

Pick something you are comfortable experimenting with; something that you identify as you, the human being.

Pause here until you have made your choice.

Advanced Thinking and Demonstrating Free Will

These are the components steps to this procedure:
1. The reflective.
2. The active.

REFLECTIVE

Do the exercise in the last chapter with one simple addition:

1. See yourself creating that fear, but not as one moment or one character. Recognise how you have created that fear in 100, or 1000, different characters that use your human form, but none of which are actually you.

2. Do this until it makes your human form laugh and feel proud.

3. Recognise how you have been using this Fear to augment your sense of human identity.

4. Because you are engaging in Advanced Thinking, you will become aware of alternative behaviour, and identities, that do not display that Fear.

ACTIVE

It is time to practice manifesting your fear in THE NOW.

This next step is incredibly effective at causing change, with little or no effort:

1. Do the reflective exercise, whilst you are actively manifesting your fear. The key to this technique is to keep recognising that you are a super-consciousness. For example, that will give you the energy surges, you should now be familiar with. You could say you are being awake in "Real Time".

2. Observe everything you have to do to manifest your fear. Doing this properly will make you laugh, and you will feel the warmth of unconditional love.

3. You will notice that manifesting your Fear requires a great deal of work, and some ridiculous behaviour.

4. By repeatedly recognising that you are a super-consciousness you will lose interest in repeatedly recreating that fear moment, BECAUSE YOU WILL HAVE EXPERIENCED IT.

You, the super-consciousness, will then create some new human experiences, instead of that old Fear.

You may have to repeat these two procedures many times, to get results. By gaining experience with simple fears, they will give your human form the practical ability to demonstrate Free Will, with your more exciting challenges.

The Great Simulator In Action

At the beginning of Part 1 of this book, it was pointed out to you that you were experiencing an amazing illusion.

If you have been successfully practicing the exercises given, you will be seeing yourself in an entirely different way. It may only happen for a few minutes, now and again, but it will be happening, and these minutes will become far more frequent.

To begin with you will have perceived most of what happens to you, as being the result of some outside force. Now, you will be recognising that you are the creator of that force. You will also know that it is pointless imagining this, you can only know it.

Experiencing The Great Simulator is a fantastic opportunity; make the most of it.

26 Simulator Summary

Summary Of How The Great Simulator Works

Nothing written in this book is a theory. It is merely an observation that you can test for yourself.

Basic Design

You, the super-consciousness, want to "see" what you really are. The best way to really see anything is to see it from a completely contrasting viewpoint. So you create a multitude of contrasting viewpoints, an infinitesimally small proportion of which are human beings.

You, the super-consciousness, have created a sort of simulator which enables you to experience being completely different from your actual self. Everything in the simulator is your creation and exists only because you wish it so.

This means that nothing in the simulator can be intrinsically good, or evil, just an alternative state from your actual self. Hence, in the simulator, there is no, "right" or "wrong", nor can there ever be; just the way it is.

Human consciousness

This is one of the many alternative states you are experiencing. A human consciousness is constructed from many components. Here is a simplified summary:

- The soul beings. They closely resemble you, the super-consciousness. They also create the manifestation of a higher self. You use these entities to inspire what manifests in The Great Simulator.

- The guiding spirits or Guides. They are largely responsible for enabling a human consciousness to experience a higher awareness. They also determine a human being's principal skills. e.g. A musically talented human being will has musically talented Guides.

- The Special Effects Team. This incorporates an incredible multitude of spirit entities. Their main job is to produce the impression that a human being, or human spirit, actually exists. They produce the bulk of all the thoughts and emotions a human being will ever experience.

The vital point to note is that a human consciousness is constructed from lots of elements. The mix of what constitutes a human consciousness also changes from moment to moment. So, in effect, it is not even actually the same consciousness that existed only a moment before.

The most amazing thing about a human consciousness, and the human form which results, is that it generally believes itself to be an independent entity. It has the capability to experience itself as separate from you, the super-consciousness. Considering that you, the super-consciousness, is everything, this is an amazing feat of "spiritual engineering".

The human consciousness actually believes that it is alive and, to a large extent, "on its own". It thinks that it is real. In the upper regions of heaven which approximately equates, subject to how you define anything, to the Middle Astral, the human consciousness does recognise that it is not independent, and is actually part of you. However, on the Earht plane, it experiences so many low vibration energies that it tends to believe that it is a human being.

The human consciousness also, generally, fails to recognise that it is you, the super-consciousness, which is ultimately experiencing everything that happens to it. By this means, you can experience praying to yourself for help, as if you needed to be informed about what your human form was undergoing.

To put it another way, you are experiencing not being yourself. This allows you to experience a massive contrast, from which you can recognise what you really are.

Human challenges

You often create a human consciousness and give it a solitary life, such as, a hermit on a mountain top. For this human consciousness to recognise what you are is relatively easy, because it does not have much else to do.

More challenging is to see if you can recognise what you are from the perspective of, say:

- A single mother of five children.
- Holding down two part-time jobs.
- And further distracted by a drugs and alcohol addiction.

Perhaps, in a "perverse" way, this is going to be far more interesting and fun, as accomplishing this challenge is:

1. Much harder.
2. Also has a greater degree of the all important contrast.

Creating human challenges

A human being is DESIGNED to believe that it does not want to have to experience many of the challenges it faces.

You, the super-consciousness, have given your human consciousnesses only one way to escape the challenges they face. Human consciousnesses have to pay attention to what they are, in the process of which you recognise what you are.

The degree to which a human consciousness has to recognise what it is and, hence, what you are, is generally quite minor, in respect of completing any particular challenge. The design of The Great Simulator is such that these recognitions are "incremental". From a human perspective this could be understood as:

1. Adding up progressive moments of awareness.
2. Undertaking progressively more difficult challenges.

This is really not complicated to understand, as the principles behind The Great Simulator are actually very simple.

Working with human challenges

A "Cosmic Joke" is that human beings are, endlessly, preoccupied with attempting to dispense with their challenges, whereas they really only exist to undergo them in the first place. It's no wonder that human beings occasionally form the view that they were born to suffer.

When a human being basically "stops complaining" and pays attention, it does actually handle its challenges competently; because that is what it was also designed to do.

Human beings can do whatever they want

Actually they can't, because they have no Free Will of their own (see previous chapters and next section). In the meantime, they can go through the motions of doing whatever they like:

- They can be pleasant to each other.
- They can kill each other.

There is no need for one human being to force another human being to do anything.

Ultimately, human consciousnesses all, discover for themselves that they have no real alternative to paying attention. Forcing them to do so only gives them something to rebel against, and thus delays their development.

Free Will

This book is designed to assist human consciousnesses experience Free Will.

No Free Will

A human consciousness that is not paying attention has NO Free Will whatsoever. It cannot escape the challenges it faces, because you do not want it to.

A human being facing an apparently difficult challenge could, for example, commit suicide. That human consciousness, having removed the illusion of having human form would then experience the following:

- It would to some extent recognise what it was; i.e. You.

- It would then remember that it wanted to experience that challenge in the first place.

Normally, it would then want to "have another go" at, more or less, the very same challenge it had previously tried to escape. Hence, it will normally want to reincarnate back into human form with a similar life path.

Round and round

Human consciousnesses that return to the heavens recognize rapidly and re-experience, their Earht plane adventure from the perspective of a higher awareness. When they recognise what really happened, whilst also experiencing more of what they really are, they frequently desire to undergo a similar experience again. Hence they reincarnate, albeit in a slightly different form.

After all, they are doing no more than recognising what you actually want.

Solution under your human nose

Because this is a summary, I am only going to remind you, the human consciousness, that if you are paralysed by the "heavy energy" of a challenge......... It is that same energy which will provide you with a solution.

Do not fight it. It is there to help and enlighten you.

Accessing Free Will

Human beings, generally, wish to be free of certain challenges you have given them. What they mostly fail to recognise is the perfection of why that challenge existed in the first place.

All challenges are designed to be solved by becoming more aware, and then applying that higher awareness to behaving differently on the Earht plane. Resolving these challenges, by other means, causes them to recur, possibly with new variations.

A simple way to resolve any challenge is to:

1. Remember what you actually are (see previous exercises).

2. See the perfection of why you created that challenge in the first place.

Now seeing the perfection has a very interesting effect. You may not, upon recognising what you actually are and what you are up to on the Earht plane, actually want to terminate a particular challenge.

3. Work with that challenge. This tends to solve it, though frequently not in a way a human consciousness might have initially anticipated.

4. Simply be more aware of what you are, whilst working with that challenge.

5. When you can do this, to whatever standard of competence you have set yourself, you no longer have need of that challenge. You will stop creating it.

Here is how you manifest Free Will.

6. When you have completed whatever awareness exercise you set yourself, then you can set yourself a new challenge, to keep your human consciousness occupied.

7. What that challenge will be is up to you. You, the super-consciousness, are in charge.

This is the same exercise that was given in the last chapter. Practice it.

Checklist

Recognising the difference between *being* aware and *thinking* you are aware can be difficult. This is because a human consciousness has a tendency to imagine that it is aware. Furthermore, as being aware requires deploying the same senses you use to imagine things, you need to instead notice the greater reality around you. You really do have to pay attention.

If that wasn't difficult enough, a human consciousness can flip between being aware and being asleep, very quickly. So you could be experiencing being highly aware one moment, only to go into a "walking sleep state" the next, while still imagining that you are very aware.

People who remember their nightly dreams will know that it is very difficult to recognise that you are dreaming because:

1. You are in an even lower state of awareness.

2. You human consciousness will keep trying to make sense of what you are experiencing and to convince you that your dream is real.

Fortunately, there are clues to your lack of awareness. Personally, I found myself in just such a situation the night before writing this section. I was dreaming that I had been swimming fully clothed. When I got out of the water, most of my clothes were still dry. That was my clue to recognise that I was in fact dreaming.

Similarly, whilst you, the human consciousness, are going about your daily business in a "walking sleep state", there are plenty of clues that you are in a low state of awareness.

Here is a list of things you could be aware:

1. Stupid mistake

Not doing the higher awareness exercises. This is both the most common and the stupidest mistake of them all, but, as the world is perfect, it is also a manifestation of an intention to "go through the motions" of developing a human consciousness, whilst actually successfully staying asleep.

2. Noticing the difference

As previously observed, the "miracle" is that your human consciousness makes it possible for you to believe that you are the same person, from one moment to another. So, for example, as a human adult, you will tend to think that you were the same person that you were as a child.

This means that, as you practice the exercises, you will, simultaneously, experience a sense of being "the same person" who had never practiced them in the first place.

So when you practice the exercises, don't be fooled by any false sense of "getting nowhere". This is something you are likely to experience even though you will be considerably advancing your higher awareness and Advanced Thinking ability.

Be more aware of the real differences you are achieving.

3. Back-to-front world

When you are using your higher awareness you will notice that the Earht plane is a very "back-to-front" experience. Often things are different, or even completely opposite, to the way they may initially appear.

4. Humour and Unconditional Love

Being serious makes the illusion of human existence stronger. "Serious" tends to imply that there is a problem that needs to be solved. A serious attitude, or thinking pattern, allows you to deny that you created that problem, entirely for your own benefit, in the first place.

A simple test, of how serious you are being, is to be aware of how funny you find the challenges you have created. This is not to suggest that you should laugh at, and then ignore them. Do that and those same challenges will simply re-appear, until you do pay attention.

If you stop taking your challenges seriously and, instead, see them as excellent opportunities to improve your greater awareness, and human abilities, then they are your friends.

In this situation you can embrace them with the unconditional love they deserve.

So are you experiencing the unconditional love ?

5. I am Creating versus Things happen to me

One of the biggest illusions, you are experiencing, is the appearance of things happening to you that you do not appear to have created. Most human consciousnesses experience the impression that "life is happening to them".

To be fair, you did want to experience things appearing to happen to you, in the first place. After all, that is what the Earht plane is designed to do.

What you will start noticing, more and more frequently, is that you are also the creator.

6. Imagination versus Awareness

A human being will spend a great deal of time fantasising. This is often categorised as “thinking”; Such use of senses is, in fact, imagination. Human consciousnesses do this, principally, because they experience a dislike of themselves and their perceived situation.

The illusion The Great Simulator generates is, largely, possible because human beings spend most of their lives lost in imagination, of one sort or another. Breaking out of the illusion simply requires more unconditional love, and noticing where you actually are.

7. Are you noticing something very basic ?

Are you noticing that the human entity you are inclined to think you are, is just an illusion ?

This is something you cannot imagine. After all, using your imagination is part of the illusion you are experiencing in the first place.

As you practice noticing, you will get glimpses of the greater reality, then you will return to experiencing the illusion The Great Simulator provides.

With practice, the glimpses become more frequent and longer.

8. Guides

If you are not aware of their presence, you are probably busy imagining something.

Are you practicing your Astral awareness exercises regularly ?

9. Special Effects Team

Similarly, if you are not aware that the thoughts and emotions your human consciousness is experiencing are created by the Special Effects Team, then you are asleep.

10. Going Nowhere

I, personally, find this a very entertaining one. On Earth I can appear to be walking down the street. If I raise my awareness, I can see that my human consciousness is actually going nowhere. It makes me laugh.

11. Time

If you are perceiving time as basically linear, you are not in a very aware condition, so pay attention to the time.

12. See Yourself

This is the only thing you have to do (actually, it is an option with no ultimate alternative)......... Whilst living a full and demanding human existence, with the highest level of competence and awareness.

Have fun and see you soon.

In Part 3

Part 3 of The Great Simulator will assist your development of Free Will by comprehensively covering the following three areas.

1. Stepping out of the most self-limiting philosophy a human being can ever experience.

2. Lots of practical tips you can apply to increasing your awareness, and hence physical capability, on an everyday basis.

3. Many useful examples that will give you powerful insights into your own human life.

To give you a little more detail:

1. The most self-limiting illusion

Is that there is something fundamentally wrong with you. You are perfect. You simply wanted to experience what it is like to feel imperfect and occasionally even a failure.

Surprisingly, the principle, that there is something wrong with you, is one of the defining philosophies that govern most people's lives. If you think this does not affect you, then you are fooling yourself. Our modern urban society is completely orientated to make this limiting illusion a normality.

Here is how you can easily spot that you are being affected. How often are you afraid to do:

- The things you want to do ?
- That would also benefit others in a win-win way ?

You will no-doubt already have rejected the principle, advocated by many religions that you are fundamentally sinful, as it is merely a cunning system used to coerce and control you. Now it is time to recognise that society, as a whole, is limiting you through a more subtle application of the same bogus principle.

Stop excusing your lack of action in doing the beneficial things you want to do.

2. Practical tips

That will accelerate your development. In Part 1 you were given an outline of how The Great Simulator operates. In Part 2 you were given practical techniques that enable you to start to see The Great Simulator in action for yourself.

However, "one size does not fit all". Everyone is unique, and so are your personal requirements. If you have the possibility of doing some personal training on this subject, that is the best solution but, as that may not be an option, for whatever reason, then in Part 3 I have detailed many of the common difficulties people face, along with practical techniques to overcome them.

3. Examples

Realistically it was not possible to include the vast wealth of examples at my disposal, in either Parts 1 or 2. Furthermore, in the absence of you having actually practiced the exercises outlined in this book, it would have been difficult for you to fully appreciate many of them.

Here is a selection of the sorts of examples we will be looking into:

- How previous incarnation have affected others.
- How previous incarnation might be affecting you.
- Astral Projection experiences.
- Places you should visit on the Astral.

- The ghosts all around you.
- Ghost busting.
- Working with guiding spirits.
- Healing.
- Life changing experiences.
- Curses and unpleasant forces.
- Advanced Thinking solutions to practical challenges.

Part 3 will be terrific.

It will give you a wide variety of techniques that will help your Free Will take another leap forward.

The only possible catch:

If you are reading this in 2007, I am sorry to inform you that Part 3 will not be available until 2008. However, if there is some subject that you would like covered in Part 3, and you contact me prior to publication……… Your request might just get included.

To get your copy of The Great Simulator Part 3
(Or to add your name to the waiting list)

VISIT THE WEBSITE AT:

www.Great Simulator.com

Do you know the contact details for:

Gareth Williams **(in Ireland ?)**

The last time I physically saw Gareth Williams was in Dublin, Ireland, in July 1997. A combination of his amazing spiritual teachings and devious antics helped inspire me to leave the country and move to the UK.

At this stage, much of the personality I knew then has been dismantled and replaced with something new. However, I would like to make contact again with Gareth and discover the finer points of the new entity he has evolved into.

If you know the contact details for Gareth Williams:

1. Please email me at: David@GreatSimulator.com
   With the heading: Gareth Williams
   Include anything helpful: His Phone No, Address, Email, etc.

2. If appropriate, please ALSO contact Gareth and ask him to email me at the above email address with the heading: Gareth Williams.

Thanks for helping me rediscover this old friend
David

Your View

How helpful have you found this book ?

Please can you write me a review or a testimonial.

1. Let me know how helpful this book has been for you ?

2. How have practicing the exercises changed your life ?

3. What benefits have you experienced ?

Please email me at: David@GreatSimulator.com

With a subject / heading line of: Testimonial
Or
Review

Thank you
David

PS.
As this is a first edition book there may be the very occasional typing error. If you find one, or something similar, that you think I would like to be made aware of, then please email me ***separately*** at the above address with a subject line of: Typo
Thank you.